DAVID ISAACS

AN ACCIDENTAL ACTIVIST

CONTENTS

Alick and Susanna Isaacs

CHAPTER ONE: WHAT SUSANNA KNEW

My earliest childhood memory from August 1953 is of my twin brother Stephen and I being on the first floor of our house in our father's arms watching a taxi pull up in front of our house. Our mother got out of the taxi, holding a bundle. I remember thinking to myself, "What's the old girl gone and done now?" What she had done was have a new baby, our sister Harriet. Stephen and I were a month shy of our third birthday. Our view of Harriet was obscured by vertical wooden bars, inserted after a toy elephant went through the window. The bars were to assure that no more toys or even boys "went through the window."

My mother had the opportunity to win £100 with a £5 bet if she had twins. My father, the scientist, said the odds of a pregnancy being twins were 80:1, and there was no family history of twins, so dissuaded her. Of course, when we turned out to be twins, people came out of the woodwork remembering that Aunt Mabel and Great-Aunt Agatha had had twins. Susanna often teased Alick about what they could have done with £100.

We lived at the end of a cul-de-sac in Finchley Central, North London (there was a song by The New Vaudeville Band called "*Finchley Central*": it starts "Finchley Central is two and sixpence from Golders Green on the Northern Line"). Our parents allowed us to play naked in our garden, but we were not allowed to go up the quiet suburban street naked. Stephen and I devised a plan to hang our shorts on the gateposts either side of the front gate. If we wanted to play up the street, we would grab the shorts and put them on before running up the street.

Susanna, Alick, David and Steve

Stephen and his wife Mary still live in Finchley Central; my wife Carmel and I and our first two children lived a mile away in East Finchley for 18 months.

Our mother Susanna's father, Hubert James Foss, was a pianist and composer, the youngest of 13 children. At age 24, he became the first ever Musical Editor for the Oxford University Press (OUP), based at Amen House in London. He built up their Music Department from scratch to become one of the major music publishers of the early 20th century. Hubert published works by the most important English composers of the time, including Ralph Vaughan Williams, William Walton and Peter Warlock, and was instrumental in promoting performances of their works. He was not a fan of Benjamin Britten's work and did not recruit him. Hubert helped Percy Scholes publish what would be the first edition of *The Oxford Companion to Music* in 1938. Hubert gained some renown as a composer, including setting *Seven Poems* by Thomas Hardy to music for baritone solo. His most famous achievement was to arrange J. S. Bach's aria *See What His Love*

Can Do for keyboard (for organ solo and for two pianos), a piece Susanna adored and had played at Alick's funeral. Susanna was named after the character of Susanna in Mozart's comic opera *The Marriage of Figaro*, but Bach was always her favourite composer. Incidentally, William Shakespeare and Anne Hathaway had a daughter Susanna (as well as twins); William Shakespeare was one of my mother's great heroes.

Hubert's elder sister Josephine Foss ("Auntie Jo") was a missionary and English teacher who, in 1914, co-founded the Pudu English School in Kuala Lumpur, where she became headmistress. She encouraged the girls to play sports, as a way of freeing them from traditional gender roles. In 1942, when the Japanese invaded Malaysia, Auntie Jo was imprisoned in Changi Prison. Her personal memoirs describe the harshness of the conditions, including 12 kilometre walks in the heat and humidity of the day; some soldiers had to be picked up by trucks, but tiny Auntie Jo persisted. In family folklore, Auntie Jo had memorised entire Shakespeare plays, and organised her fellow prisoners to put on performances. When she was liberated, Jo was severely malnourished. The American soldiers gave her an egg, the first she had seen in four years. But Jo was made of stern stuff. She recovered, went back to teaching in Malaysia and lived to a ripe old age.

When she retired, Auntie Jo lived in London. One day she found a painting in her attic, which she put in her handbag and took to the auctioneers, Christie's. "Where did you get this painting, Madam?", they asked suspiciously. It was by Francesco Guardi, the 18th century Venetian grand master. She gave it to Hubert and Dora's son, Christopher Foss, as a wedding present when he married Nora Kelly.

Susanna's mother was Kate Carter-Page. Kate came from a family which for many generations owned nurseries and were seed merchants. Kate was a red-haired beauty. Susanna described her mother as impulsive, promiscuous and wilful. Hubert and Kate married in 1921, when Hubert was 21 and Kate 20. Susanna was born on April 11th 1921, so Kate was already pregnant when she married Hubert.

Kate's brother, Peter Carter-Page, was a famous puppeteer who designed and built his own marionettes. I remember Stephen and I being taken to visit Peter in his puppet theatre. We watched him manipulate the marionettes, and I was entranced by the dark red velvet curtains framing the stage, the glamour and the theatricality of it all.

Susanna's sister Elisabeth was always called Timi, apparently because when her sister cried, Susanna would say: "What's the timi matter?" Timi was born 14 months after Susanna. Susanna always suspected Timi did not have the same father as her. Timi was very short-sighted and Sue would often tell us that she thought Timi's father was the poet Edward Thomas, who was notably short-sighted. There was a family connection: Kate's brother Geoffrey married Edward and Helen Thomas's daughter Bronwen. Only after Susanna's death did I realise that Edward Thomas was killed in World War I in 1917, but Timi was not born until 1922. Susanna's notion about her sister's parenthood was pure fantasy. However, Timi's daughter Susie Robson tells me that Timi's father might have been Merfyn Thomas, Edward's son.

Susanna's enthusiasm for music exceeded her ability. She was an ordinary pianist and could not sing in tune. In view of her mother's promiscuous nature, maybe Susanna was worried that Hubert was not her father.

When my mother was two years old, her father left the family home. My mother and Timi were told he had died. They did not see their father again for four years, which is when they heard he had been alive all that time, living nearby. Apparently the injunction that Hubert should disappear was in the terms of the separation, but telling his children that he was dead was a cruel thing to do and had a long-lasting adverse effect on my mother and her sister. A similar thing was done to John Lennon, who was told his mother was dead when she was living nearby. Lennon never got over it.

Susanna was a very observant child. When Susanna was

18 months old, Hubert, Kate, Timi and she lived briefly in the picturesque village of Otford in Kent. Over thirty years later, she and Alick were driving in Kent and took a detour to see Otford. Susanna told Alick she remembered the village. Alick doubted her memory. Susanna told him that when they drove round the next corner he would see a thatched cottage with a climbing yellow rose on the left. Sure enough her memory of the cottage from less than two years of age was absolutely accurate.

One time, Susanna's parents hosted a visitor who was pregnant. Susanna, aged about 4, told the pregnant woman that her fetus was covered in hair. Susanna knew because she had a book about pregnancy. History does not relate whether or not the woman was glad to know this information about her fetus, but Susanna had made an early statement about her future medical career.

Hubert married Dora Stevens, a soprano, and had two further children, Susanna's half-brother and half-sister, Christopher and Diana. Christopher Foss owned a bookshop on Baker Street, not far from Sherlock Holmes's fictional house. Diana became a schoolteacher and married Brian Sparkes, a Professor of Classics at Southampton University. Kate died in 1952 and Hubert in 1953, before my sister Harriet was born. I don't remember ever meeting either of them.

Kate married Dr Edgar Obermer, an endocrinologist. They were part of the Bloomsbury Group (or Set) which included Virginia Woolf, E. M. Forster, Lytton Strachey and John Maynard Keynes. Dorothy Parker said of the Bloomsbury Set: "They lived in squares, painted in circles and loved in triangles." Henry James was an American author who settled in London and became part of the Bloomsbury Set. His book *What Maisie Knew* eerily evokes the same sort of uncertain childhood that Susanna experienced.

At one point, Edgar, Kate and family lived in Manchester Square, an 18th century garden square in Marylebone, London, close to where Charles Dickens had lived. Edgar had two children by a previous marriage, Ruth and Jim. Ruth and Jim took jujitsu lessons. That is, until the day Ruth and Jim returned from a lesson just as Edgar was saying goodbye to a patient in the front hall. Both Edgar and the patient were thrown to the floor. That was the end of jujitsu lessons.

Like Mr Micawber in Dickens's *David Copperfield*, Edgar always lived beyond his means. He would owe increasing amounts of rent until, all of a sudden one day, he would tell the family they would have to leave their house immediately. The children were not allowed to return to their room to retrieve any of their possessions. For this reason, Timi took to wearing a purse around her neck containing her most valuable treasures. Timi continued to wear a purse round her neck until the day she died, in her seventies.

Kate's mother May and her father "Gramps", a seed merchant, lived in Thorpeness, a seaside village in East Suffolk. They often looked after Susanna as a baby. They had no space for a cot, so put Susanna down to sleep in the empty bottom drawer of a chest of drawers. Susanna was always devoted to Granny May and to May's great family friend "Auntie Minnie". In later years, Susanna would visit Auntie Minnie in Thorpeness, but could not keep up with her as Auntie Minnie, in her eighties, sped across the rocks.

When Susanna was 5 years old, she and Timi were sent to the experimental Malting House Garden School in Cambridge. The school was set up in 1924 by English journalist and educationalist Geoffrey Pyke in his own home. It was run by a famous psychologist Susan Isaacs. Susan Isaacs was no relation of Alick, but he would often tease Susanna that she only married him for his name. Ruth and Jim also went to the Malting House. Timi cried all the time. Jim would not learn to read. He loved cars and Susanna would read him a magazine called Autocar. Eventually she got fed up and told Jim he would have to learn to read it himself, which he promptly did. Susanna, Timi and Jim only went to the Malting House for two terms. Susanna and Jim then went to King Alfred's School, near Hampstead Heath, for a short while, a school to which my twin brother and I also went some 30 years later.

One day, Edgar sat on a hot water bottle which burst in the bed, scalding Kate badly. Edgar, who was a controlling man, refused to take Kate to hospital for treatment and pain relief, insisting that he would look after her at home. He gave her morphine. When Susanna was 12, she was searching through her mother's chest of drawers for something when she discovered a drawer full of needles and syringes. Susanna realised that Kate was a drug addict, which explained some of her more erratic behaviour. Presumably, Kate's addiction resulted from the morphine Edgar gave her.

Life was hard for Susanna and Timi, Ruth and Jim, until Edgar and Kate decided to send them to a progressive, co-educational boarding school in Devon, called Dartington Hall School. Leonard Elmhirst, a Yorkshire-born agronomist, born in 1893, had married an extremely wealthy American heiress, Dorothy Whitney. Dorothy Whitney's first husband Willard Straight died in 1918, age 38, from influenza during the global "Spanish influenza" pandemic. Their daughter Beatrice Straight, who became a Hollywood actress, was later responsible for bringing Anton Chekhov's nephew Michael Chekhov to teach drama and artist Mark Tobey to teach art at the Art School which Leonard and Dorothy established at Dartington.

Leonard, who originally intended to enter the Church like his father, studied history and theology at Trinity College, Cambridge, in his own words getting an honourable third (the lowest pass). However, he then moved to Cornell University, Ithaca where he completed a four year course in agriculture in two years. He met his future wife Dorothy while fundraising for a club which supported foreign students. Leonard must have made an international impression. In 1921 (the year my parents were born), Leonard was invited by the Bengali poet and Nobel laureate Rabindranath Tagore to accompany Tagore to India. The aim was to set up a model village promoting the humanities and an Institute for Rural

Reconstruction at Santiniketan, West Bengal.

Returning to England at the time of the Depression, Leonard and Dorothy set up a similar rural experiment to Tagore's, but at Dartington, a place Tagore knew and had recommended. The roof of the ancient manor house, Dartington Hall, had caved in. In replacing it with great beams of timber from the estate, Leonard and Dorothy helped form Staverton Builders, the leading builders in the South-West of England. The ancient art of glass-blowing, once well-known in Devon, had been lost. Leonard and Dorothy sought 16 skilled glass-blowers from Sweden, who came and taught the necessary skills to the locals. Thus was born Dartington Glass. Weavers were encouraged and Dartington blankets became highly sought after. Timi and her husband Pete gave Carmel and me a Dartington blanket as a wedding present; we still have it and treasure it. The Elmhirsts' philanthropy transformed Dartington from a sad, Depression-plagued village with high unemployment to a thriving country village with high rates of employment.

Dave, Harriet and Steve

Timi became a Communist and married another Communist Peter (Pete) Robson. Timi and Pete lived in a top floor flat in a run-down apartment block near White City. Pete worked for the railways and a large proportion of his salary went to the Communist Party. We visited them often. When I was doing biology at school, we were asked to test our family for tongue-rolling, a dominantly inherited trait. Pete could not roll his tongue, which "proved" biologically that he could not be the father of any of his three children. Timi was amused, not worried, and Pete worked out that he could not roll his tongue with ease because he had suffered a gunshot wound to the jaw during the war.

One summer holiday, Timi and Pete took Stephen, Harriet and me with their three children John, Bill and Susie to stay in Wales with them. They had obtained the use of a disused train which sat stationary on a railway siding. The train had railway carriages with bunk beds. We children vied for the top bunk. At least until I fell out of the top bunk onto my head. Luckily I did not lose consciousness. We were by the sea and spent hours rockpooling, suffering sunburn which caused Susanna to scold Timi, unfairly I thought. The children all took a bus into the local seaside town where we played arcade games. We miscalculated and did not have enough money to pay for all the bus fares back, so Johnny crept onto the bus with his knees bent and a cheeky grin on his face, having persuaded the driver to let him on half fare. Johnny taught us the famous John Lynch song:

She stood on the bridge at midnight
Throwing snowballs at the moon
She said 'Sir, I never 'ad it'
But she spoke too bloomin' soon.
It's the same the whole world over
It's the poor what gets the blame
It's the rich gets all the pleasure
Ain't it all a bloomin' shame

As Pete became increasingly disillusioned with the Communist Party, he quit his job with the railways and retrained as an electrician at a technical college. He then was hired to teach trainee electricians at the same technical college. Pete had been under the illusion that the rich, which included my parents, did not have to work hard for their money. That illusion was shattered when Pete started teaching.

Pete's increased salary allowed them to buy a small brick cottage called Snail's Halt, at Pool Hill, near Newent in rural Gloucestershire. The cottage was almost completely surrounded by trees. There was a garden with a grass bank, which Anna and Ben used to run down when we visited. We stayed with Timi and Pete on a few occasions and it always felt magical to be with them.

One day, Pete told me he had ringing in one ear and was unsteady on his feet. I said it sounded like labyrinthitis, a type of ear infection, but he should consult his family doctor, who agreed. Pete always crossed the road to his technical college at a point where he thought there should be a zebra crossing. Two days after our conversation, Pete crossed the road at that point, staggered backwards and was run down fatally by a truck. He was just 64 years old. It was a horrible tragedy, and of course poor Timi and their children never got over it.

Leonard's full name was Leonard Knight Elmhirst. The Knight is a family name. The irony is that Leonard was offered a knighthood and turned it down as being incommensurate with his republican values. Leonard and Dorothy wanted a school for their own children: Dartington Hall School started in 1926. The progressive nature of the school attracted the famous to send their children to Dartington Hall School. Many of the children came from broken homes. The children of author Aldous Huxley (who wrote *A Brave New World*) and mathematician Bertrand Russell, artist Lucian Freud and his brother chef–broadcaster Clement Freud (grandsons of Sigmund Freud) and social scientist Michael Young (who started *Which?* Magazine and The Open University) all attended Dartington at the same time as Susanna and Timi. My mother was always afraid that Edgar would not pay the school fees and they would have to leave. But, recognising her potential, the headmaster Bill Curry had asked Leonard and Dorothy to give Susanna a scholarship to pay for her school fees, which they had done. Susanna did not find that out until years later, and wished she had been told. Susanna and Timi adored Dartington. As the school holidays came to an end, they would talk of "going home to school".

The school had a reputation for licentiousness, largely fuelled by the fact that children of both sexes were allowed to swim in the river naked. In 1930, the Elmhirsts appointed William Burnlee Curry as Head of Dartington Hall School. Curry had been a science teacher at Beedales, then Headmaster of Oak Lane Country Day School in Philadelphia. Curry was short, bald, and round-faced with a prominent forehead. He always had a pipe in his mouth and a twinkle in his eye. When told there was a rumour that if you visited the Hall, the butler would open the door stark naked, Curry retorted: "If he was stark naked, how did they know he was the butler?"

The English Isaacses

There was no corporal punishment at Dartington. The school was liberal and forward thinking. For example, teachers did not punish children immediately for serious wrongdoing. Instead, the consequences of children's actions were decided by the School Council, which consisted of both staff and pupils. One possibly apocryphal tale was of a young boy who kept stealing the other children's bicycles. The solution of the Council was to contribute a penny each and buy the miscreant his own bicycle. Certainly Dartington understood deprivation. Susanna was a lively, vociferous pupil. If she became too rambunctious, she was excluded from the lesson. She loved to learn, so being told she was being too naughty to be taught was a true punishment to her. What a wonderful way to teach children the value of education.

Aunt Timi

Curry had some innovative ideas. Whenever he introduced a new idea to the school, he would say mischievously: "From tomorrow there will be a tradition..." Curry attracted some illustrious teachers. Susanna had fond memories of David Lack, the biology teacher, who studied robins in the Dartington Hall gardens and wrote a famous treatise on how aggressive and territorial they were. Each male robin had his own territory and would attack any male trespassers. When Lack rigged up a tuft of red feathers on a pole, the resident robin would attack it fiercely and peck it to bits. So much for the myth of the sweet Christmas robin. Bernard Leach taught pottery and soon achieved fame for his lively, innovative pots. Imogen Holst, daughter of composer Gustav Holst who wrote *The Planets*, was the music teacher. One day, she was doing a masterclass with a young cellist. When he played the piece, Imogen criticised him ferociously. He played it again and Imogen said: "Better. Still very, very bad, but better." This became one of our family sayings; it would always cause us much mirth.

Leonard and Dorothy bought a Henry Moore sculpture of a reclining woman which overlooks the tilting yard in majestic fashion. Henry Moore became a friend of the Elmhirsts. Many years later, Leonard and Susanna would visit him in Carrara, Italy, the place where Michelangelo sourced his marble. Henry Moore had a house near the Carrara marble quarry. Italy gave Henry Moore free marble in honour of his global stature.

Years later, when Susanna was in a wheelchair, our great friend Judith Gibbs took Susanna, Carmel, Steve and I to Henry Moore's farm Hoglands in Perry Green, Hertfordshire. I pushed Susanna around the exhibition and the sculptures. It was a memorable day.

Dartington Hall had a medieval tilting yard where knights used to joust, from the early 14th century onward. The sides of the tilting yard had steep banks flattened off every few yards, so they were like giant steps. The tilting yard and the steps had deteriorated over the years, but were renovated when the Elmhirsts bought Dartington Hall, and are now as smooth as velvet. One magical night, the famous Indian sitar player Ravi Shankar and his troupe came to play at Dartington Hall. The pupils sat on the grass steps. It was night-time; a huge cauldron sent sparks soaring into the air. It was one of my mother's most vivid memories evoking the magic of Dartington.

Every Sunday morning, Leonard walked round the Dartington Hall grounds and called in to visit the staff. One such Sunday, Leonard stopped to visit one of the workmen and his wife, but Leonard's arrival scared a rook that was nesting on the chimney. The rook's flight dislodged part of the nest, which fell down the chimney and landed on the living room floor, scattering twigs and soot everywhere. The poor workman and his wife were mortified at the mess. But Leonard got down on his hands and knees in his Sunday best to examine the débris, saying "Oh great. I've always wanted to know what rooks use to make their nests."

Dartington Hall and tiltyard

Dartington steps and tiltyard

Even after Susanna left school and had a family, most of our summer holidays were spent in Dartington. I remember our family having afternoon tea with Leonard and Dorothy Elmhirst on the lawn at Dartington Hall. Leonard was impressed that I, aged 8 or 9, knew the names of the birds that we saw, nuthatches and tree-creepers. My father had taught me on walks on Hampstead Heath.

Susanna would often say that Dartington saved her life. Sadly, it could not do the same for Jim Obermer. Edgar's relationship with Kate did not last. Jim and Ruth went to Switzerland with Edgar, staying in the mountains above Lake Como for a while. Then they returned to England; nothing lasted long. In 1942, Sue was told Jim had been killed in an accident during military training. But she knew in her heart that was not the truth, and soon found out that Jim had been at his grandfather's house in Lewes, Sussex when he cut his wrists and drowned himself.

Ruth Obermer moved to Los Angeles where she trained as a nurse. She lived there for the rest of her life. In her later years, she was visited and succoured by Susanna's grandson (Stephen and Mary's youngest child) Jonni and his husband-to-be Tim Lubina. Ruth died peacefully at the age of 90.

My mother was the first pupil from Dartington Hall School to go to university. She was admitted to Bristol University to study medicine. She was a fast runner and played hockey on the wing for the university. She had very little money, and earned pocket-money by reading Dickens to the elderly father of Bridget Edwards, a Dartington teacher. Bridget Edwards never married but we had no grandparents, so we asked her to be our adopted grandmother. Bridget accepted with a broad smile. When Bridget was living in a retirement home, Susanna was living in California, so Carmel and I used to visit Bridget. When Bridget was dying, Susanna flew from The United States to be with her. Bridget held on and died within minutes of Susanna arriving at her bedside.

When she finished her pre-clinical medical training at Bristol, Susanna was in such straitened circumstances, she thought she might have to give up studying medicine. But she won a prestigious Rockefeller scholarship to complete her clinical training in Chicago. She travelled in a convoy, it being World War II. She asked why two ships kept signalling each other. She was told the captains were playing chess. What she was not told was that the two last ships in the convoy had been torpedoed and sunk. Her ship was the next in line.

Chicago was an education for Susanna. One day, as a Rockefeller scholar, she was invited to dinner with the Chancellor. The Chancellor's chauffeur, who was black, picked Susanna up and drove her to the dinner. When they arrived, my mother thanked the chauffeur. The chauffeur was stunned; he told her that nobody had ever thanked him for driving them before. A Jewish dentist told Susanna that he would never use an instrument in a white person's mouth which he had previously used in a black person's. He had separate sets of instruments for black and white patients. My mother certainly saw racism first hand in Chicago.

Susanna returned to England to do her final examinations. In Bristol, an orthopaedic surgeon examiner asked her how she would treat acute osteomyelitis (bone infection). "With penicillin, if I could get hold of it", she said. "Rubbish. New-fangled nonsense, it'll never catch on", said the orthopaedic surgeon and failed her. Out of pique, Susanna decided to do her final MB examination in London instead of Bristol. The examination was held in the Royal College of Surgeons. My mother asked for the ladies' toilet. There wasn't one. They had to write a label LADIES and pin the label on one of the men's toilets. My mother was doing a physiology practical examination and was trying in vain to dissect a frog's leg and get a nerve to fire. A man came round saying: "Where's candidate 92?" The man was Professor Samson Wright, author of the leading physiology textbook of the day. "That's me", said my mother with trepidation. "You got the highest mark in the physiology written exam, my dear", he said. "That won't be any use, because I'm about to fail the practical", she said. "Oh nonsense", he said. "Let's just fiddle with this", and he got the frog's nerve firing in no time.

In the clinical viva, one of the examiners handed Susanna a specimen jar containing an insect and asked her what it was. "A bed bug", she said, rather embarrassed. She had seen many of them in Chicago. The examiner hooted in triumph. "Someone's got it right!", he called to his fellow examiners. "What diseases does it cause?", he asked. "I haven't the faintest idea," said my mother. "Nor do I", said the examiner.

Susanna passed her London final MB examination with honours. She was now a qualified medical practitioner. As a junior doctor, Susanna worked at Shadwell in the East End of London near the docks. Drunken sailors would often be brought in half-drowned after falling off the gang-plank leading back to their ship. Susanna lived in the hospital and did not have a day or night off for a year, although the doctors were rarely called at night. One day, she was having a sandwich between seeing patients in the Emergency Department, when a patient walked by. "Oh, you eat", said the patient. Doctors were seen as not quite human, both by their superiors and by their patients.

Some doctors were truly not quite human. One of the consultant surgeons had a reputation for being short-tempered. Susanna was assisting him apprehensively during an operation when, in her nervousness, she dropped an instrument on the floor. "You bloody idiot," he shouted at her. "I didn't bloody do it on purpose," she shot back. "No, you didn't, my dear," he conceded. From that moment onward, he treated her with the utmost respect throughout her internship.

Susanna decided to study paediatrics, which she did in London, at Great Ormond Street Hospital, and in Sheffield under renowned paediatrician Professor Ronald Illingworth. Illingworth was the author of a major paediatric textbook called *The Normal Child*. According to Susanna, Illingworth and his wife Cynthia, also a paediatrician, had a number of children and he would write a new edition of the book every time they had another child and his view of normality broadened. This was a Susanna exaggeration: the Illingworths had only three children whereas the book extended to ten editions. But it was a good story, often repeated by Susanna.

One day in Sheffield, Susanna was unwell and had to go to hospital. A junior doctor in a white coat made a dreadful hash of trying to take a blood sample. When he finally succeeded, he said, "And what do you do for a living?" When my mother said she was a paediatric senior registrar, he winced and rushed out. He must have come back, because that young man was my father, Alick. Clinical medicine gave Alick an ulcer, so he had decided to become a scientist. Perhaps he was doing a bit of clinical work to earn some money. His main occupation in Sheffield was to work with Sir Charles Stuart-Harris, a world expert on influenza viruses and the first person to show that influenza was different from common cold viruses. Years later, I was asked by my dear friend Tony Delamothe, deputy editor at the British Medical Journal (BMJ), to review a book on interferon written by Dr Robin Stuart-Harris, Charles's son. My father Alick discovered interferon in 1957. Robin was an oncologist interested in the therapeutic effect of interferon on malignancies. The title of his book is *Clinical Applications of the Interferons*. I called my BMJ review: "Son of Interferon meets Son of Influenza". After the BMJ review was published, Robin came round to my house with a kind gift of a framed photograph of his father with my father. I had never seen the photograph before.

Alick was the eldest of four children born to Louis and Rosine in the moderately affluent Glasgow suburb of Pollockshields. However, previously Louis and Rosne had lived in the poor, slum area of Glasgow called the Gorbals. Alick's ancestors fled Lithuania around 1880, at the time of the pogroms against the Jews. When there was a pogrom, around a third of young Jewish men were killed, a third were made to join the army, and a third were forced out of the country. Our family name in Lithuania was Galinsky, but the British customs officer could not spell it. He asked Alick's paternal grandfather what was his name. "Barnet", he replied. What was his father's name: "Isaac". So Barnet Galinsky became Barnet Isaacs.

Louis worked in the furniture business. Alick was apparently his father's favourite. Although professing to be a devout Jew, Louis would take Alick out for non-kosher meals as a supposed treat. Alick was already having doubts about religion when, at age 13, he had his Barmitzvah, the Jewish coming-of-age ceremony. He was appalled how people who barely knew him competed to give him the most expensive presents. He swore to himself then that he would never follow the Jewish faith.

Alick studied medicine at Glasgow University, winning many medals and prizes. He was a medical student during World War II, and did not enter the military. Alick's brother Bernard also studied medicine and went on to become Professor of Geriatrics in Birmingham, England. Bernard was renowned for the community and social approach he brought to geriatrics. At a PBAC meeting, I asked the geriatrician if he knew of Bernard Isaacs. "Oh, Isaacs of the four I's you mean: intellectual impairment, incontinence, immobility and instability (falls)." I have tried to emulate Bernard's approach by teaching junior doctors that they should be interested in their patients, be inquisitive and be sensitive.

Having made a name for himself as a promising young virologist, Alick was invited to Melbourne to spend a year at the Walter and Eliza Hall Institute (the WEHI), working under the aegis of immunologist Sir Macfarlane Burnet, a future Nobel Laureate in medicine and physiology. Alick and Susanna were courting. While Alick was in Melbourne, he and Susanna wrote to each other every day for a year.

Alick's work was on viral interference, the phenomenon that infection with one virus can interfere with and prevent infection with a different virus. Burnet assigned Alick a laboratory technician, but often asked the laboratory technician to come and do experiments with him, even when Alick was in the middle of an experiment. When asked to give a talk to the other laboratory scientists at the WEHI, instead of talking on his topic viral interference, Alick just called his talk "Interference".

After Alick had been in Melbourne for a year, Burnet asked him to stay for a second year. Although they knew it would cause ructions with Alick's family, Alick and Susanna decided to get married in Melbourne.

Susanna worked her passage to Australia as an assistant ship's surgeon. The real ship's surgeon was drunk by mid-morning every day, and Susanna lived in fear she would have to operate on a passenger. In the event, she was only called upon to operate on some chickens which ate too many stones and became crop-bound (blocked oesophagus). Apparently, chickens have very few nerves in the neck, so Susanna could open the chickens' gullets, scrape out the stones and stitch up the chickens' oesophagus and neck, causing minimal pain. Louis sent frequent abusive messages to Susanna on the ship, accusing her of ruining Alick's life. The purser would say "Sorry, doc", and produce yet another poisonous message.

When she reached Melbourne, Susanna worked as a registrar at the world-famous Royal Children's Hospital, while Alick continued his research at the WEHI. They were married at Melbourne Town Hall and honeymooned in the Blue Mountains. Coincidentally Carmel's parents honeymooned there in the same year.

Alick's father Louis was aghast that his eldest son had defied him. Louis ordered the family to "sit shiva" over Alick. Shiva is a funeral service, so the message to Alick was that he was dead to his Scottish family. Many years later, my son Mark entered into correspondence with one of Bernard's sons, who was named Alick after my father. Alick said that his father Bernard felt dreadfully conflicted about the shiva, with his loyalties divided between his father and his elder brother. Bernard remained angry all his life about what Louis did to my father and about the pressure that Louis put on his other children to comply with his vindictive actions.

Susanna was pregnant with twins when she and Alick left Australia. When Stephen or I wanted to tease our sister Harriet, we would sometimes say "We've been to Australia". "No, you haven't, you were just in Mummy's tummy", she would protest. On their return to England, Alick and Susanna lived in London. Alick worked as a virologist at the Medical Research Council building in Mill Hill, which had a green roof. Alick cycled to work each day. He had a briefcase clipped on the back of his bicycle. He was quite absent-minded, and the briefcase was forever falling off. The police would bring it round with a grin: "Dr Isaacs's briefcase again".

Susanna trained as a child psychiatrist and as a psychoanalyst, following the teachings of Melanie Klein. My father used to go to wine-tasting classes. One day, he came back grinning, saying that a woman had come to the class who knew a lot about wines. Alick got talking to her. She was Melanie Klein.

Stephen and I were the first grandchildren on both sides of the family. When we were born, Rosine told Louis that she was going to London "for a shopping trip". Louis knew his wife well enough not to argue and not to enquire further. Sadly, we saw very little of Rosine and Louis, both of whom were dead before Harriet was born, as were Kate and Hubert. We would sometimes visit Hubert's second wife Dora, a soprano, who would sing and play piano, and her children Christopher and Diana in their house in Hampstead Garden Suburb.

Soon after Stephen and I were born, Alick came to the hospital to visit Sue and us. "They've put the twins in the wrong cot", said Alick. "I know", said Susanna. "I don't want to disturb them". I am impressed that Alick could tell the difference between us immediately. I struggle to tell other identical twins apart. But being different people is so important for twins. My mother was reading Donald Winnicott on twins, and Winnicott emphasized the importance of ensuring that each twin was an individual, that they were not just "the twins". Initially my mother used to dress Stephen and I in identical clothes. That is, until she read Winnicott on twins. And until Stephen and I started looking at our reflection in the mirror and saying the other twin's name. Thenceforth, not only did she dress us in different clothes, but she sewed a "D" and an "S" on our trouser pockets. If anyone asked Stephen or me our name, we would point to the letter on our pocket and say, scathingly: "Can't you read?"

Before Harriet was born, our parents took us on outings, one parent with one twin. Then the next outing, Alick and Sue would swap and take the other twin, ensuring we each spent quality one-on-one time with both parents. People would often give Stephen and me identical presents. We would always swap them, and from that day on, we could always tell which present belonged to which one of us, for example through minute scratches invisible to anyone else. We were as keen as our parents to avoid favouritism.

Stephen and I must have been hard work as children. As infants and toddlers, our parents used to put one of us in the playpen and the other outside, so we didn't fight. As we became verbal, when our mother told one of us off, the other would say: "Go on, kick her." One day, Stephen and I knocked a treasured china mixing bowl off the table, breaking it. "Why did you do that?" asked our stunned mother. "To see if it would break," was our answer. "I could have told you that," she said. When Alick came home and Susanna related the story, his response was: "Hooray. They're going to be scientists."

On another occasion, our mother took us to visit an old friend in her seaside cottage. They were drinking tea in the downstairs kitchen. Stephen and I, aged about 3, disappeared upstairs. My mother was concerned about the possibility of damage; her friend reassured her there was nothing upstairs we could damage. After a while, my mother said: "It's awfully quiet up there." When we started giggling, they checked. Stephen and I had gone systematically from room to room taking out the plastic slats used in all the gas fires to transmit the heat, and breaking each slat into multiple pieces. Our friend was very magnanimous. She said it was her fault because she was the one who said there was nothing to be damaged upstairs.

We had a cat called Grace. Our mother used to put baby Harriet in her pram in the front garden to get some fresh air. One day Grace scratched the new baby. Our parents sent Grace off to the vet to be neutered. Steve and I were impressed that we might be sent away if we hurt the new baby. There but for the Grace of God went us. But, disaster, Grace died under the anaesthetic. Mortified, our parents told us that Grace had gone off to live with the vet. A few months later, she overheard 3-year-old Stephen ask me: "What *did* happen to Grace?" "Oh, she died, of course", I said. "Oh yes," agreed Stephen. Maybe you were executed if you hurt the new baby.

When we were 3 years old, Alick's host in Melbourne, future Nobel Laureate for Medicine Sir Macfarlane Burnet came to visit our family in our London house. Stephen and I challenged him to play dominoes with us upstairs in our room. After half an hour, Burnet came back down the stairs looking puzzled. "That game is just luck, isn't it?" he asked. "They cheat", said my father.

Our mother indulged Harriet (although in Stephen's and my opinion, she "spoiled" Harriet). Susanna's stated reason was to compensate Harriet for not having a twin to play with. On reflection, the true reason may have been that Susanna was trying to compensate herself for being deserted by her father when she was two years old. Of course, Stephen and I resented the favouritism and would often tease Harriet, as older siblings do. There was a family photograph of Harriet, aged about one, sitting on the grass crying. Stephen and I are sitting either side of her each holding one of Harriet's arms. After the photo had been taken, Steve whispered to me: "Were you pinching her arm?" I admitted to it, and he said he was pinching her too.

Our parents almost never smacked us, but one mealtime I had gone too far, so my father smacked my bottom and sent me to my bedroom. Stephen carried on being difficult. "Do you want your bottom smacked too?" he was asked. "Yes," he said. So my father smacked his bottom, too and sent him to the same bedroom.

One time when we were about seven years old, Stephen and I were fed up with our parents. We decided to get up at midnight and run away to live on Hampstead Heath for three nights. I have no idea why three nights. We prepared so carefully that we even hid a toilet roll in the old gramophone in our room. But on the night we planned to leave, Stephen felt ill and told our parents: "I have a confession to make." He told them of our plans. "What's wrong with home?" asked Alick. "*You*," said Stephen. The reason he felt ill was that he was covered in chickenpox spots.

On another occasion, at about the same age, I sat on the stairs and said to Alick: "It's my right to be a Catholic if I want." I have no idea what prompted that comment, especially as both my parents were atheists. I do think it is interesting that I was already speaking the language of rights at age seven. My parents were amused, but a bit agog, too. As fate would have it, Stephen and I both married devout Catholics.

Harriet coud be amusingly scathing with her mother, Susanna. One time when she was cross with Susanna, Harriet said of a meal: "It's horrible and anyway there isn't enough of it." On another occasion, Harriet said to her mother, "You do plough a very narrow furrow".

Neither Alick nor Susanna were very politically active. In the 1950s and 1960s, however, every Easter, huge crowds would gather outside the Atomic Research Establishment at Aldermaston in Berkshire and walk 52 miles to London to protest against nuclear weapons. These were called the Aldermaston marches. Alick took us children with him for the last day of the Aldermaston march on a couple of occasions.

Stephen and I had a toy trolley with a bar to pull it along; we called it "the battle wagon". Stimulated no doubt by the Aldermaston march, we used to go to Hampstead Heath carrying signs saying "Ban The Bomb". One time, we took a young friend with us; when he got home he insisted to his parents that we wanted people to bang the bomb.

Dave and Steve set up chairs at Dartington

CHAPTER TWO: HAMPSTEAD

We were a happy family. We moved to a large house just ten minutes walk from Hampstead Heath, yet 20 minutes drive from the city of London. There was a significant family connection with Hampstead: Alick's mother Rosine lived happily in Hampstead as a child. On weekends, our father would take us on walks on Hampstead Heath. Stephen and I would pretend the grey squirrels we saw were engaged in battles with red squirrels, although in truth there were no red squirrels on the Heath. Alick would point out the different birds: jays, long-tailed tits, nuthatches and tree-creepers. When I was 9 years old, I gave up my plan of being an ornithologist, realising that there was only one David Attenborough. I had always enjoyed holding a baby on my lap. I decided that I would become a paediatrician, like my mother. I also decided I liked the sound of being a Professor.

Alick had a Morris 8 car. He did not use it often, preferring to cycle to work. In the winter months, he would often have to use a crank handle to start it. It was a reliable car. It could drive us the 220 miles from Devon for our holidays, although that journey took over 8 hours in those days.

In the middle of the week, Alick would go for a walk on the Heath with a close friend, the epidemiologist Jerry Morris. They would go to a pub called Jack Straw's Castle on the edge of the Heath. It had ugly mock battlements and was nowhere near as sophisticated as another pub on the Heath, The Spaniards Inn, which Keats used to frequent, but which was a bit too far away. Alick and Jerry would go into the pub for a drink, leaving Steve and I to sit on a wall outside with a packet of potato crisps each. Alick was not a big drinker, even when unwell. We never saw him drunk.

Hampstead had something of a village atmosphere. We had a lodger called Patsy who was an actor. Patsy was in a play with a boxer dog called Linda. At the end of the production, Linda had nowhere to go and was going to be put down. Patsy pleaded with our parents, and hence Linda became part of the family. Stephen and I adored Linda. Patsy was an enthusiastic gardener, and our parents were happy for her to work on improving our garden. There was a horse stable near our house, and the horses would be taken for a walk to Hampstead Heath early in the morning. I can still hear the clip-clop of their hooves on the road. When she heard the sound of the horses' hooves, Patsy would leap out of bed and rush after the horses with a bucket and spade to scoop up horse manure. Our roses were magnificent, but the garden did whiff a bit.

At the front of our house was an incongruous Victorian marble statue of a naked man, almost life-size, carrying off a naked woman, presumably representing the Rape of the Sabine Women. The statue came with the house. When we were about 5, Stephen and I used to find ladybirds in the garden and race them upwards from the man's toes. The winner was the one whose ladybird first reached the woman's buttocks. One morning the plinth was bare. Thieves had come in the night and stolen the statue. Our parents gave the police a photo of the statue, but the police informed us that gangs of thieves operated who would transport stolen statues in trucks to Scotland and sell them. They held out little hope that we would ever see the statue again and we never did.

We children squabbled, as children will. Alick had a good sense of humour. He would try to defuse things by saying: "What's the family motto?" We had all learned to say: "It's not fair." He even got us all to draw the family coat-of-arms with the motto "It's not fair" emblazoned on it.

On weekends, our father sometimes took us by public transport to London Zoo in Regents Park or to visit one of the museums in Kensington. Once, when our father took

Harriet, Stephen and me to the zoo, he showed us a massive, dusty rhinoceros, with its thick hide and long, curved horn. "This is one of the fiercest animals in all Africa, even in the World" he told us. At that point, a woman arrived at the rhinoceros enclosure, dressed in dapper, matching tweed jacket and skirt, and carrying a bag. "Gertrude", she said in a commanding voice, "Sit down." The magnificent animal sat down. Then the lady fed it carrots from her bag. The rhinoceros crunched the carrots contentedly, dribbling frothy orange saliva. We three children took every opportunity to remind our father of the fierce rhinoceros called Gertrude.

I used to have vivid dreams of hordes of kangaroos hopping across vast red plains. Presumably my fascination with Australia stemmed from my parents being married there, and Stephen and I being conceived there. Many years later, when my wife Carmel and I were newly arrived in Australia, one of her friends drove us across their farm. There was a drought, and kangaroos hopped across red plains just as in my childhood dreams.

My favourite museum in Kensington was the Natural History Museum. I, who have always lacked any discernible sense of direction, knew my way past the skeletons of dinosaurs and whales straight to a display that housed stuffed sea creatures. There was my favourite creature in the museum, a small white baby fur-seal. I have always been keen on birds, but the static displays of birds in the museum seemed to me eerily lifeless and drab. Thus, my adoration had to be transferred to a stuffed seal cub.

Alick and Sue were great entertainers and we often had guests for lunch on the weekend. Our parents always invited overseas scientists working at Mill Hill. Irma Pick was a South African psychoanalyst, later famed for her work on the counter-transference. Irma, her husband Abe and their newborn son Daniel were preparing to leave South Africa because of their opposition to apartheid. Tragically, Abe died from pancreatic cancer shortly before they were due to leave, and Irma left South Africa with one-year-old Daniel. Irma and Daniel moved to Hampstead, a short walk from us, and came to Sunday lunch every week for years. Daniel became a psychoanalyst and Professor of History at Birkbeck College, London.

There was a family rule, "no balls in the house". One Sunday, Stephen and I were on the first floor playing an improvised game of cricket, hitting erasers with rulers. Suddenly there was a crash from below. We raced downstairs to find that a large chunk of plaster had fallen from the ceiling. The table was laid for Sunday lunch. The plaster had crashed onto the table, but had fortuitously missed all the plates and glasses.

Stephen and I briefly attended King Alfred School, a small school on the periphery of Hampstead Heath. It was two bus rides away from home, but there was no need to cross the road. Our mother did follow us the first time we made the journey to make sure we were sensible. Although we were only 4 years old, from then on our parents trusted us to make the journey unaccompanied.

In the 1950s, London was still prone to bouts of "peasouper" fog. When the fog was at its worst it was impossible to see a metre ahead. I don't remember fog like that from our King Alfred days, but I certainly do when returning from George Eliot School. Maybe the fact that Susanna was immersed in the psychoanalytic training and Alick was often not well had something to do with it, or maybe it was much quieter, but I cannot imagine many parents letting their 4-year-olds catch two buses to and from school nowadays.

When Stephen and I were 5 years old, we went to George Eliot Primary School, in Swiss Cottage, a state-run primary school. This required a single bus ride along the Finchley Road. The school was close to Lord's cricket ground. Steve and I were very competitive with each other, as I believe are many identical twins fighting for their identity. We would sometimes get into fierce fights with each other which would end with one or both in tears of rage. The head agreed with our parents' suggestion to put us into different classes. We remained in separate classes until we were 10. Classes were streamed by ability for our last two years at George Eliot. Our parents did not want to compromise our academic chances, so we were put in the same class.

Our sister Harriet went to George Eliot School 3 years after Stephen and I did. Although we often teased her at home, we were very protective of her at school. Woe betide anyone at school who bullied her.

To my shame, despite attending George Eliot School, I did not read a book by the famous author George Eliot until I was in my seventies. I fear I was unconsciously discriminating against women writers. In my seventies, however, I borrowed *Silas Marner* from the library, and found it to be a short but beautiful book. I plucked up courage to borrow and read all 950 pages of *Middlemarch.* Virginia Woolf described Middlemarch. as "one of the few English novels written for grown-up people." I had no trouble in reading it in the two weeks allotted to me. It is truly a classic.

David(ov) on the violin

When we were 7 years old, the Head announced in assembly that a violin teacher was coming during the morning break, and if we wanted to learn the violin, we should attend. In those times, tuition of musical instruments was provided free by the British government. I attended and started to learn the violin. It was 3 weeks before I said to my parents: "I hope you don't mind, but I've started learning the violin." They were surprised but thrilled. The violin classes involved several children learning at once, and were not of a high standard. After two years my parents found me a wonderful Hungarian violin teacher, Clara Toszeghi, née Bakony. In Hungary she was known as Bakony baby. Her nickname was Maxi, although she is small (now 95). Clara could have been a great soloist, except that she suffered from severe performance anxiety. However, she played chamber music and taught violin. I used to cycle to Swiss Cottage (near George Eliot School) to my weekly lessons with my violin strapped on the back of my bicycle. Unlike my father and his briefcase, I did not let my violin fall off the bike. Clara did not believe in examinations. Playing the violin should be for the love of it. What a wonderful attitude I thought then and still do. Clara organised for her pupils to play concerts instead of work for exams. I liked the violin but was also interested in many other activities such as sport. "Why don't you practice, Davidov?" she would say to me, plaintively.

Clara's husband Toni was a haematologist and general physician. He was also Hungarian, but was forced to learn Russian when Hungary was under Russian rule. It was Toni who gave me the nickname Davidov. I used to play bridge with Toni and his friends. I adored Clara and Toni, and their son Misi.

When I was about 16 years old, I needed a new violin. Clara offered to drive me into the centre of London to a famous violin shop, Beare's. As we were walking from the car to the shop, three of the Beatles crossed the road in front of us, dressed as they were for the cover of the Abbey Road album, and being mobbed by a crowd of adoring fans. It was a bizarre conjunction of pop and classical music.

Being given the opportunity to learn the violin made a huge difference to my life. In those days, I am not sure about nowadays, it was common in European countries like Hungary, Roumania and Poland, for children to learn instruments from an early age. I very much doubt that free lessons are offered anywhere in Britain or Australia nowadays. I stopped my lessons when I left secondary school, but played chamber music and in orchestras while at university. After university, I played in local community orchestras for years. My favourite was the Beecroft Orchestra, which had members from age 14 to over 90 (the 90-year-old horn player Mal Hewitt used to play for the Sydney Symphony Orchestra and at 90 still plays in perfect pitch and time). The Beecroft Orchestra conductor Joanna Drimatis was inspirational. I played with the Beecroft Orchestra into my seventies, until I became too unwell to play. I loved rehearsals as much as, or even more than, concerts. An orchestra is like a big family. I was even lucky enough to play a choral concert in the grandeur of Sydney Town Hall with The Occasional Performing Sinfonietta conducted by Mal Hewitt.

My favourite teacher at George Eliot was Mr Halfyard (it was before everything went metric). He loved cricket. If he was in a good mood he would come striding down the corridor bowling an imaginary ball. If he was in a bad mood, he would be batting with a scowl. In the classroom, if you were talking out of turn, a piece of chalk would suddenly bounce off your head. Mr Halfyard was a good shot. Well mostly. Every now and then he would say "Sorry" as the chalk bounced off the wrong head. Mr Halfyard loved geology and took us on field trips down the South coast hunting for fossils. I loved Mr Halfyard's field trips. A few years later, some of my schoolmates organised a reunion with Mr Halfyard. I found that all my schoolmates also idolised him for his infectious enthusiasm. It was marvellous to be able to tell Mr Halfyard how important he had been in our lives.

The "shiva" meant we saw very little of our Scottish relatives. We did occasionally meet Alick's brother Bernard, the geriatrician, his wife Dorothy and their boys. We also met

Alick's sister Esther, who was a social worker. Stephen and I once went on holiday with Esther's family to Arisaig, a village on the west coast of the Scottish Highlands. Esther's girls, Judith and Irene, were agog. They had never seen anything as energetic and wild as Stephen and me.

When we were 9 years old, we had a memorable family holiday visiting the Orkney and Shetland Islands, which we reached by boat after driving from London to Aberdeen. Alick was an amateur archaeologist and took us to the remarkable archaeological site of Jarlshof, which contained prehistoric remains from 2500 BC and Norse remains. Stephen and I played at being Vikings, crawling through narrow entrances and ambushing imaginary intruders. Our parents could never have persuaded us to go on a ten mile walk, but when they said they were taking us to watch seals, we walked ten miles without complaint. When we walked, if it was where the large arctic skuas nested, they would dive-bomb us, frequently causing us to throw ourselves to the ground. Skuas get most of their food by flying at gulls and terns until they drop their feed, then swooping down and catching it in mid-air. We saw them feeding this way. My most treasured memory from Shetland was walking up a steep track to the lighthouse. On one side of the hill, puffins with startlingly colourful beaks were flying in and landing at the entrance to their burrows, right in front of us. On the other side of the hill, thousands of gannets were fishing by diving vertically into the water, hitting the surface like arrows.

Stephen and I belonged to the carefully named XYZ (eXceptional Young Zoologists) Club, which was affiliated to the London Zoo. Once a month, a group of XYZ members would meet beside a big lake in Regents Park. We would count the ducks on the lake, as part of a national census. It was a bit boring counting mallards and pochards, although I remember the excitement when we saw a smew one day. We were supervised by identical twins, John and George Newmark. It was always John and George, never George and John, I am not sure why. I am ten minutes older than Stephen; maybe John was ten minutes older than George. The Newmarks were always immaculately dressed in identical tweed suits, identical woollen ties and identical moustaches. John and George were writing a book together. Each of them would write his own version of the same chapter. After the duck count, we would sit with them on adjacent park benches. They would give Stephen and I each one of their chapters to read. Then Stephen and I would swap chapters. Finally, Stephen and I would tell the Newmarks what we liked best from each of their chapters. Their book was eventually published as *To the Zoo in a Plastic Box* by John and George Newmark, which sounded suspiciously similar to Gerald Durrell's classic *A Zoo in my Luggage*. They may have hoped to attract some of Gerald Durrell's readership, but I don't think the Newmarks' sales figures threatened those of Gerald Durrell.

After reading the chapters, the Newmarks would take us behind the scenes at the zoo. I remember tiny tiger cubs which worried our feet and chewed our shoes. I remember feeding grapes to a toucan. The toucan would hold a grape at the end of its huge beak, then tilt its head back and let the grape roll gracefully into its mouth. I remember a young orang-utan called Charlie who would climb all over us and find any chocolate that was hidden purposefully or accidentally on our person.

John and George Newmark asked Stephen and me if we would accompany them on a trip to West Africa. We were very excited at the prospect, but our parents refused point-blank. They said it was too dangerous. Stephen and I thought they were concerned about venomous snakes, scorpions or lions. It is only in retrospect that we realised our parents were concerned about our going overseas with two single men they did not know. No disrespect to the Newmarks, who lived into their nineties and have now died, but I understand my parents' concern.

I used to try to go home with Shahid Hafiz, whose father was high up in the Pakistani army and whose mother always had delicious dishes simmering on the stove. Shahid had two beautiful sisters, Shameem and Shaheen, and a handsome younger brother Hamid. If I was in luck I would be invited to stay for supper. There were only two scholarships available to boys from our area to go to Haberdashers' and Shahid and I won them.

When it came to High School, our parents asked if we would like to go to different schools. Stephen and I discussed it and agreed it would probably be best for our long-term relationship if we went to different schools. Many years later when I was a paediatrician, a 12-year-old boy told me he was a twin. I asked if he and his twin were identical. "No" he said insistently. "I can't tell them apart", his grandfather interjected. Clearly the boy looked very similar to his twin, but was making the point that they were different people and he wanted others to treat them as such. I talked to him and his parents about ways of facilitating their independence, including raising the possibility of the boys going to different schools.

Our parents believed in state education, and would probably have sent us to state schools, but we both won scholarships to private schools (as did our sister Harriet later) and our parents did not want to impede our education. Stephen went to City of London School for Boys, next to Blackfriars Bridge in the heart of London. Ten years later, Mike Brearley went to the same school. Mike got first class honours at Cambridge University, became England cricket captain, and then became a leading psychoanalyst, whom Steve knows well. City of London boys had to wear caps even in the sixth form. When they left school, they all threw them off Blackfriars Bridge, launching a small flotilla of caps down the Thames.

I went to another boys' school, Haberdashers' Aske's School ("Habs"). It was started in 1690, for the sons of members of the worshipful company of haberdashers. In the 1960s, any boy could go there if their parents could afford it (or if they won a scholarship). The school was deep in the Hertfordshire countryside, near the famous Elstree film studios, so far out that coaches were provided to take us from the stations at the end of the underground lines, Edgware, High Barnet and Stanmore. Our only famous old boy was convicted of spying for the Russians. I do not know if I would have preferred a co-educational school. I rather think so. But that was not on offer.

I loved primary school, which was free of prejudice. Stephen and I once asked our mother if little Johnny could come over to play. Our mother said she didn't know him, who was he? We said he was the boy with curly hair. When he arrived he was a black African boy. We didn't notice skin colour at primary school.

However, on my first day at Habs, one of the boys asked my name. "David", I said. "No, your surname." "Isaacs". "You must be a Jew boy", he said with a sneer. "I don't know", I said, "I'll have to ask my parents." Our parents had never discussed Judaism with us, perhaps to protect us, perhaps because it was too painful a topic for them. My Pakistani primary school-friend Shahid experienced significant racism. Haberdashers had more than its fair share of antisemitism and toxic masculinity. But after the first shock, I enjoyed secondary school, largely because I loved playing rugby and cricket. I played violin in the school orchestra and I always came second in the annual music competition, which was always won by a wind ensemble (and deservedly so). At the end of my first year, there were exams, and I won four prizes, all books I had chosen including the Complete Plays of William Shakespeare. The other boys asked how much revision I had done. None, I had never heard of revision. Subsequently, I did moderately well academically, but the only other prize I won was the maths prize for "O" (Ordinary) level elementary mathematics, when I got 92%s and 100% in the two papers. A far cry from my maternal grandmother who once got every question wrong in a mathematics exam but was given 2% for neatness. Alick liked mathematics and used to play games of mental arithmetic with us. While I was good at elementary mathematics, I struggled with advanced mathematics and was pleased to drop it for "A" (Advanced) levels.

Our parents were avid theatregoers. When Stephen and I

were 13 years old they went to the theatre without us, to our annoyance. That night I dreamt I was on the train to school. When the train reached Edgware, everyone got off. But as the train reversed into the siding, there was one lone boy left staring forlornly out of the window. His name was Nick Woolf. The play our parents had seen was *Who's Afraid of Virginia Woolf*. If I ever doubted the existence of the subconscious mind, surely this provided sufficient proof.

The first Shakespeare play to which our parents took us children, all three of us, was *Romeo and Juliet*. Stephen and I were 10 and Harriet 7. Harriet wept buckets, but later became a teacher of English and drama. The part of Juliet was played by Judi Dench. I was in love and have been a devoted fan of Shakespeare and of Judi Dench ever since. When we were 17, Steve and I drove our parents' car to see Judi Dench play the part of Sally Bowles in *Cabaret*. Afterwards Steve and I waited at the Stage Door. When Judi Dench emerged, I offered her a lift. "You cheeky young man", she admonished me, laughing.

While I was at Haberdashers, I auditioned for plays, but to my chagrin, was told I was too short to be considered for a major part. When I was 15, I was an extra and played the violin in a school production of *Romeo and Juliet* which played at Habs, and then toured several towns in Germany. I remember being entranced by the ancient Bavarian town of Aschaffenburg. I also remember vomiting on my school uniform after drinking too much German beer.

Our parents loved classical music, although when they went to classical music concerts, Susanna was sometimes so exhausted that she would ask Alick to take her home at the interval. Every Easter they would go to a performance of Bach's St Matthew Passion at London's Royal Festival Hall, a tradition Susanna continued for years after Alick's death.

One day, Stephen and I decided to swap schools for the day. We chose the last day of term, because little work was usually done on that day. We each picked one friend, told them our plan and asked him to take our twin around for the day. Steve's friend was George Wilde, mine was Phil Ind. Steve and I told very few people at school that we were twins, harking back to Winnicott stressing the need for twins to each develop their own identity. The day of the swap went without a hitch, apart from the Latin exam I had to take at Steve's school. I didn't learn Latin, but I copied from George Wilde. None of the boys at either school noticed anything amiss. However, on the first day of the next term, I was approached by my maths teacher, Mr Darcy. "You were very rude to me on the last day of term", he said. "I have an excuse", I said. "It had better be a good one", he said. "It was my identical twin brother, not me", I said. "That is a pathetic excuse", he said. "Except it's true. Ask Phil Ind. He showed my brother round." Years later, I was invited back to Haberdashers' to give a careers talk to the boys. Almost every teacher stopped me and said, "I remember you. You swapped schools with your twin brother for a day." So we entered school folk lore, probably at both schools. My Curriculum Vitae included: "David has an identical twin brother, Stephen. They went to different schools and once swapped schools for a day".

At 14, the school offered me and some other boys, including Phil Ind, to skip a year and go straight into the 5th form. I decided to skip the year, but I struggled, particularly with physics, which I needed, along with biology and chemistry, to qualify to study medicine at university. In the examinations at the end of 5th form, a year from my final examinations or "A" (Advanced levels), I got 21% for physics. My father was ill and my chemistry teacher, whom I liked, had drowned in the school holidays. I decided to repeat the year and did a bit better in physics next time. One advantage of doing "A" levels early was that I was told I had to study English Literature, for a more rounded education. I studied *The Loved One* by Evelyn Waugh, *Goodbye to Berlin* by Christopher Isherwood, *Memoirs of an Infantry Officer* by Siegfried Sassoon, and the best poetry of the First World War poets. Wilfred Owen's poem, *The Parable of the Old Man and the Young,* is the most powerful poem I have ever read. Owen suffered "shell-shock" (we would call it post-traumatic stress disorder), and was admitted to Craiglockhart War Hospital in Edinburgh for treatment. He was discharged from hospital, was sent back to the war, and was killed in the last week of the war. His pre-war poetry has been compared to that of Keats. What poems he might have written if he had survived the war. I never cease to be thankful that none of my immediate or extended family has been directly exposed to a war. However, Carmel's late father George was a tail-gunner. George never talked to his family in any detail about the war, yet all his life suffered from anxiety, which I suspect was war-related.

In my last two years at Haberdashers', a young man came to join us who had previously been at Mill Hill School. His name was Nigel Calvert. He was a big man, so with typical schoolboy humour, he was given the nickname of Twiggy, after the pencil-thin model of the 1960s. Twiggy dubbed me Little Davie. Twiggy and I played in the same rugby team and rapidly became close friends. He was an excellent actor and played Sir John Falstaff in *Henry IV Part 2* and John Proctor in *The Crucible* by Arthur Miller. He was brilliant in both. Twiggy and I often used to sit under a tree in a Hertfordshire field and talk. In a short time he became my best friend. Unlike my son Mark, whose best friends were those he made in secondary school, I had few close secondary school friends (Shahid Hafiz, Philip Ind, Mark Kissin). It was only with Twiggy that I talked about feelings. My closest and most lasting friendships were forged at university and medical school.

In my later years at Haberdashers' I was a prefect (meaning I got to wear an ill-fitting voluminous blue gown), Captain of my House (called Meadows) and Vice-Captain of the school. The only job of the House Captain was to hand out lost property at the end-of-term meetings. Embarrassingly, quite commonly some of the lost property turned out to be my own property.

When I was 16, we went on a family holiday to the Arles coastal region of the south of France. Arles was an old bullfighting town but, unlike in Spain, the bulls were not killed. One day our family went to a bullfight. At one point, a challenge went out to the young men of the town. A bull had a garland of flowers tied between its horns. If any young man could grab the garland they would win a prize. While a clown distracted the bull, lots of young men entered the ring and lay on the ground, having been assured the bull would not attack them if they lay flat. I joined them. The bull stalked about, snorting but not stepping on the youth. The bull was a few metres from me. I lifted my head and could see the garland. I lunged forward to grab the garland, but the bull lowered his head and whacked me in the mouth. Fortunately, the bull caught me with the hard bone between its horns, not with either sharp horn. I flew through the air in what I am told was a graceful somersault, landed on the ground and stayed still, my mouth already starting to swell. The bull passed me by, and I hurried to the fence and exited the bull-ring. I escaped with a seriously swollen mouth, but kept all my teeth. It was the hardest I have ever been hit, much harder than any rugby field knock. A local boy managed to grab the garland, adding insult to injury.

In the summer holidays before Steve and I sat our "A" levels, Susanna, Stephen, Harriet and I drove to County Clare, Ireland. We camped on an isolated promontory, Susanna and Harriet in one small tent, Stephen and I in another, and a third tent for supplies. Stephen and I revised during the day, lying in our tent. One wild and stormy night, the supply tent threatened to blow away. Stephen and I were mortified to hear in the morning that Susanna and Harriet had rescued the supply tent stark naked. It was an image we did not want to conjure up. Susanna decided to give up camping, and we spent the rest of the holiday staying in a small, cosy local hotel.

One evening, Stephen and I drove Harriet and the hotelier's daughter to a dance. It was in a village hall ten miles away and many of the locals were walking to the dance; we fitted as many as possible into our car. When we arrived at the dance, the band had been playing for an hour, but all the young men were congregated down one side of the hall and all the young ladies down the opposite side. The four of us started dancing immediately, which acted as a trigger. All the young men crossed the floor, selected the girl they had their eyes on, and the entire dance floor was soon covered with dancing couples.

When we got our "A" level results, Twiggy had done relatively poorly. He asked if I would drive him round the country trying to get him a place at university. I had a Mini and a will, and Twiggy and I set off. His main hope was Durham, so we went there first. Twiggy has a wonderful smile and a great gift with words; he could charm anyone. I don't remember where we stayed and where else we went, except that we tried St Andrew's University in Scotland, and the police kicked us off a St Andrew's beach at 5am because we had slept there overnight. It was a great adventure, rewarded by Twiggy being offered an undergraduate place at Durham University.

Dave and Steve

CHAPTER THREE: ALICK

Alick loved working at Mill Hill. There was a wonderful collaborative atmosphere and a great sense of fun. There seems to have been none of the competitive rivalry illustrated, for example, in James Watson's book *The Double Helix.* Watson and his colleague Frances Crick appeared to resort to fairly underhand means to obtain data, along the way to delineating the structure of DNA (deoxyribonucleic acid). Proving the structure of DNA seemed more of a competition than a collaboration. Watson, Crick and Maurice Wilkins won the Nobel Prize for their work, but there remains controversy about whether they used invaluable data from Rosalind Franklin without her permission.

When Alick told his colleagues that Susanna was expecting twins, one of them said: "That damn fool Isaacs always did do his experiments in duplicate". As Lady Luck would have it, that colleague's carefully planned third and last child turned out to be twins. Alick found a periodical on family planning in the library and sent it to his colleague, marked "Urgent".

In 1956, Alick was working with a visiting Swiss scientist Jean Lindemann on viral interference. Lindemann described the atmosphere in the laboratory as very relaxed:

Alick would whistle arias and the other scientists had to try to identify them. Isaacs and Lindemann did an experiment that proved that cells infected with an inactivated virus could produce a soluble protein that could protect other cells against viral infection. They called the substance interferon and, in 1957, published their findings in a prestigious journal. Interferon explained viral interference. Furthermore, some cancers were caused by viruses, so interferon had the potential to treat some viral infections (e.g. hepatitis C was treated with one type of interferon until less toxic antivirals became available) and some cancers (e.g. hairy cell leukaemia was treated with interferon, which is still sometimes used for this indication). It turned out that there was more than one type of interferon, and that interferons modulate the immune system in important ways. Min Jin Lee, author of *Free Food for Millionaires* and *Pachinko*, wrote how she developed life-threatening chronic liver disease with cirrhosis, but was cured with three months of injections of interferon (presumably she had hepatitis C, although she does not elaborate on the nature of her chronic liver disease). The discovery of interferon was a major scientific achievement. Alick was elected to the prestigious position of a Fellow of the Royal Society. I have been told by his colleagues that, if Alick had not died so young, he would probably have been awarded the Nobel Prize for Medicine and Physiology.

Mind you, the Americans did not believe the discovery at first, of course because it was not made by an American. They even referred to interferon as "misinterpreton". Two things changed their perception. Firstly, an American scientist Sam Baron came to Mill Hill to work in Alick's lab. Sam was able to repeat Alick and Jean's experiments himself, and took the news back to the United States. Soon there were many US laboratories working on interferon. Secondly, the popular comic strip Flash Gordon showed a hero dying from a mystery viral illness. A doctor cries out: "This could be it. INTERFERON. It knocked out the virus in the lab animals." The hero is given interferon and recovers miraculously. Now even the American public had heard of interferon.

Interferon made Alick's name. He was invited to meetings all over the world, including Africa. On his return from a lecture in Africa, Alick was showing the family photographs. One was of a little girl naked except for a string of beads round her waist. "There's Africa", said my sister Harriet. She thought Alick had been to see another little girl called Africa.

First human use of interferon revealed in Flash Gordon comic strip, 1960

When his mother Rosine died, Alick became extremely depressed. Presumably the "shiva" separation contributed significantly to Alick's depression. For 3 months from 1958–9, he was unable to work. I remember coming home from school and finding him sitting on the edge of his bed sighing, even crying occasionally. Sometimes he cut his wrists, although with a blunt knife. But he recovered, and returned to work. He even taught himself Russian so that he could communicate with the Russian scientists who were experts on influenza viruses. Alick was renowned for his infectious enthusiasm, keen sense of fun and generosity of spirit.

When he was not depressed, Alick was a lively but gentle, highly intelligent man whom everyone seemed to love. He was gregarious and would talk to anyone in his high-pitched Scottish lilt. He was extraordinarily well read, both scientific and non-scientific books. Alick read all seven volumes of *À la recherche du temps perdu* ("in search of lost time") by Marcel Proust. I idolised him. Alick would always do the washing-up, so I would dry the dishes and put them away. That meant I could spend precious time with him, whether or not he was in the mood to talk.

One of Alick's colleagues at Mill Hill, and a close friend, was Lesley (Les) Baruch Brent. Les was from an observant but not orthodox Jewish family in Germany. His father had been awarded the Iron Cross in World War I. Due to racial persecution, Les was forced to leave his school in 1936, aged 11. He was sent to a Jewish orphanage in Berlin, which saved his life, because the director nominated Les to leave Germany on the first ever *Kindertransport* to England, which left three weeks after Kristallnacht. Les never saw his parents and sister Eva again. Years later, Les went to Berlin and discovered that his parents and Eva had been transported to Riga in packed cattle trucks, taken into the woods and shot. Les went to a progressive school in Kent, learned English, worked as an assistant in a chemistry laboratory to earn money, joined the British army, then studied zoology at Birmingham University. His supervisor, Peter Medawar (later knighted), persuaded Les to do a PhD with him. When Medawar moved to Mill Hill, Les accompanied him. Medawar had seen a pilot who had been shot down and sustained bad burns. Medawar was fascinated by how a skin graft from an unrelated person would take initially, then be rejected. In 1953, Les, working with Medawar and a post-doctoral fellow Rupert Billingham, showed that immunological tolerance – the capacity to accept an unrelated tissue transplant – could be induced experimentally. This won them lifelong fame. They were nicknamed "the Holy Trinity" by American immunologists. We now take it for granted that organs can be transplanted even from an unrelated donor so long as the recipient continues to take drugs that suppress the immune response, e.g. kidney, liver or heart transplants. This was unthinkable in the early 1950s.

In 1960, Sir Peter Medawar was awarded the Nobel Prize for his life work on immunological tolerance, jointly with the Australian immunologist Sir Macfarlane Burnet (for his work on the clonal selection theory of antibody production). Medawar generously shared the not inconsiderable prize money with Les Brent and Rupert Billingham, writing: "I wish to make it absolutely clear that it is in no way a present but comes to you as of right." Les Brent went on to become Professor of Zoology at Southampton and then Professor of Immunology at St Mary's Hospital, London.

Most holidays we would go to Dartington and stay in the Old Postern, originally a medieval hall house, but converted into living quarters. We would swim in the sea and attend concerts in Dartington Hall, as part of the annual Summer School. The most memorable for me were those by the world-famous Amadeus Quartet. Dartington was still like home to Susanna, and Alick lacked a home from home. It was a long drive in the Morris 8, some eight hours to reach Devon. Alick drove, while we sang songs and played word games. We would always break the journey at the Common Cold Research Unit in Salisbury, near Stonehenge. We would have a cup of tea and one of the more mechanically minded staff would fiddle with the Morris 8 to make sure it could do the distance. The Common Cold Research Unit, run by the Medical Research Council, was a series of Nissan huts left over from World War II, which had been re-conditioned for comfort to house volunteers, who were given colds by the staff, then studied. Alick knew the staff, including David Tyrrell, who first discovered coronaviruses, while working at Mill Hill, and who later became Head of the Common Cold Research Unit. David Tyrrell conducted one of the last studies at the Common Cold Research Unit, before it closed for ever, a brilliant study which showed that, if volunteers were given an identical dose of the same virus, those who had experienced significant recent stress (e.g. death of a loved one, a house move, a divorce or separation) were twice as susceptible to infection as those with a low stress score. Years later, I myself would be lucky enough to work with the great David Tyrrell.

Alick was not a practical man. He was pampered in Glasgow and never had to fend for himself. When Sue and he were marrie, he even asked her who would polish his shoes. She said "Who do you think?", so Alick polished the whole family's shoes for the rest of his life. Our mother said Alick could inoculate an egg yolk with a virus suspension with the utmost precision but he could not change a lightbulb. He did some house renovations, but said afterwards that our house was held together with Polyfilla. One day, Steve and I whose room was on the top floor, called out mo our mother "Daddy's come through the ceiling. Sure enough, one leg had appeared through our ceiling. Alick was laying down insulation in the loft and did not know that you were not meant to step between the joists.

Alick never taught us practical matters, so Steve and I never learned. One day Steve decided to mend the family vacuum cleaner. He unscrewed the wrong bolt and the working part fell on the floor, short-circuiting the vacuum cleaner and blowing up the television and the washing machine, which were on the same circuit. Mary forbade him from further home repairs, saying they couldn't afford it.

The first time we went overseas with Alick was when he was invited to speak at a conference in Copenhagen. He took the whole family, Stephen and I aged 9 and Harriet aged 6. Stephen and I played tennis. Red squirrels would sometimes approach the court, the first we had ever seen. Copenhagen had a famous amusement park called the Tivoli Gardens. In the day, classical musicians played open air concerts. There was a stall which had rows of plates. Patrons paid to throw wooden balls at the crockery and break it. There were no prizes, just the fun of shattering china. One time, Stephen and I asked to go on the roller-coaster. An adult had to accompany us. Our mother reluctantly agreed to be the one. The ride was steep and we all three arrived back white and with gritted teeth. Alick made a light-hearted comment and laughed. I remember thinking, "Oh no, don't laugh, Dad." Susanna let him have both barrels. But that quarrel was an exception. They were a loving couple, devoted to each other.

When Alick was just 42 years old, tragedy struck. In the middle of the night he awoke with a crushing headache. He was admitted to University College Hospital, London with a suspected sub-arachnoid haemorrhage. Scans showed he had bled from a congenital arteriovenous malformation deep in his brain. It was not amenable to surgery, meaning Alick would forever live with a Sword of Damocles hanging over his head: the fear that he might have another bleed. For a man whose brain was such a vital part of his life, it was a terrible blow.

As soon as Alick regained consciousness, he was in the grip of a full-blown manic episode. To this day I am unsure whether the mania was caused by the bleed itself or by the knowledge of what the bleed signified, and I am unsure what role genetic predisposition played. Whatever the cause, Alick's behaviour was totally out of character. He would shout and even throw things. By chance, the great neo-Darwinian scientist J. B. S. Haldane was in hospital at the same time as Alick. When we came to visit Alick, he introduced us to Haldane and told us that he planned to move our whole family to India for him to collaborate with Haldane. That was the mania speaking.

Alick was diagnosed with bipolar disorder, the same illness that plagued Virginia Woolf and caused her to drown herself. My mother told us that in his autobiography, Leonard Woolf wrote movingly about Virginia's illness, but I have never been able to bring myself to read it. For the next three years, Alick's mood oscillated between mania and depression. When he was manic, he would be admitted to a mental hospital, Horton Hospital in Epsom, Surrey, for weeks at a time. It was a long way from our house and we would only visit him on weekends. He would often say hurtful things to our mother when he was manic. He was also violent sometimes, which was totally unlike his normal gentle self. One time when he was at home and manic, he threw a heavy glass beer mug against the wall and it shattered. We felt as if our life was shattering.

As he became less manic, Alick would become much more normal. Mill Hill were incredibly accommodating, thanks I believe to the wonderful Head, Sir Christopher Andrewes. Sir Christopher loved Alick. He also loved butterflies. One time we went to Sir Christopher's house in the country; he gave Stephen and me butterfly nets and we went collecting butterflies for his collection. Sir Christopher appointed Alick as Head of his own Laboratory for Research on Interferon. When he was getting better, Mill Hill would encourage him to come back to work, because it was therapeutic for Alick. They gave him all the sick leave he needed.

After a period of relative normality, however, Alick would sink into a slough of despond and become severely depressed. We all feared suicide. Susanna kept working and held the family together. Alick would cycle through mania to depression and back to mania over months. When well he remained quite productive, and published some important papers on interferon.

In 1967, Alick aged 45 years, was in the bathroom at home when he collapsed. Stephen and I, aged 16, tried to help him to his feet but he was unconscious. Alick had suffered a second cerebral bleed. He was taken by ambulance to hospital but never regained consciousness. Poor Harriet was only 13 years old. Susanna made the decision for the three of us children that we should not accompany her to visit our dying father in hospital. I have often thought about that decision and wondered if it would have been helpful or harmful to see Alick just before he died.

I was deeply conflicted about my father's death. I was sad to lose my father who, at his best, radiated energy and goodwill, and brightened up the lives of all those who met him. I adored, even worshipped that Alick. But the three years of his bipolar disorder had been so devastating that there was some relief for his family, and surely for Alick himself, that we would not have to go through his mania and his depression any more. My ambivalence was not a subject I ever felt able to discuss with my mother or my siblings. Alick's death was even harder for poor Harriet, but I was in the grunting stage of male teenage communication then. Our mother sent us to school the day after Alick's death. I did not tell a single schoolfriend that my father had died. In retrospect, I see what a poor communicator I was, like many awkward teenage boys, but I also did not want to cry in front of the other boys. Twiggy, whom I would have told, did not yet attend my school, and I had no truly close friends. I would acquire my closest friends at medical school and university. I remember Alick's funeral, including the Bach cantata "*See what his love can do*", which was arranged for keyboard by my maternal grandfather, Hubert Foss, but I don't remember crying much at the funeral. I was in denial; it took me a year before I was truly able to grieve for my father.

Alick Isaacs holding David and Stephen after receiving an honorary degree

CHAPTER FOUR: FRANCE AND ITALY

Stephen and I already had a place at Clare College, Cambridge to study medicine, but we stayed on an extra term at school in 1967–8, supposedly to work for a scholarship or exhibition. These are university awards, which carry prestige but not much emolument. Stephen distinguished himself by gaining an exhibition. I was more intent on graduating from being second XV rugby union captain the previous year to playing for the first XV. I was also preoccupied with winning my "colours", which consisted of a badge awarded at the end of the season to the leading first team players to be sewn onto one's blazer. For some reason that badge had assumed great importance to me. In the event, I played the whole season as scrum half, and did not miss a game, even though I was hospitalised overnight with concussion after being deliberately kicked in the head when I lay helpless under a ruck. A cheap shot. Luckily, we did not play again for two weeks after I was concussed. I played against Stephen's school; we were both scrum half, and scrapped like old times. At the end of the season, I won my colours, but deservedly did not get an exhibition or a scholarship. Stephen's school stopped playing rugby union a year later and switched to soccer after a boy died in a rugby scrum.

This left Stephen and me nine months before we started at university. Our mother had the brilliant idea that we should work overseas in virus laboratories, but in different countries. Not only did she have the brilliant idea, but she also did all the legwork, contacting Alick's erstwhile colleagues to arrange for Stephen and me to work with them. I loved French at school, so my mother found me a position working with Professor Charles Chany in the virus laboratory at the Hospital for Sick Children,

Paris. Stephen was very good at Latin, so Susanna arranged that he work with the charming Professor Italo Archetti in Rome.

We were paid a small living allowance, barely enough to live on, but we were too proud to ask our mother for money and too keen to demonstrate our independence. Stephen soon learned Italian and supplemented his salary by translating scientific papers from Italian into English. I was not as resourceful, and found myself "down and out in Paris", like George Orwell. I was often very hungry and, when I took the metro, I would stare longingly at the vending machines. I had one decent meal a day. That was lunch, which we laboratory technicians cooked on bunsen burners and ate in the laboratory. That practice would certainly not meet current occupational health and safety regulations. It is amazing what staff could do in 1968.

Having very little money, I visited museums with free entry. In the famous Tuileries Garden, I discovered a museum called the *Jeu de Paumes* which housed a small collection of paintings by various impressionist painters. Immediately opposite was a small gallery called the *Orangerie* which contained nothing but large paintings by Monet called *Les Nymphéas,* the water-lilies. I visited these museums many times. It was the start of a lifelong love of the impressionists.

A friend took me to the *Musée Rodin*. It consisted of a small garden tucked away in an obscure part of Paris, such that it felt as if we were in the country. The garden was full of some of Rodin's most famous sculptures, including *The Thinker* and *The Burghers of Calais*. I did not like them very much, but the setting was magical.

My most unlikely find was the *Musée de Cluny*, a museum in the city centre of Paris, on the corner of the *Boulevard St Germain* and the *Boulevard St Michel*. The exterior of the museum was packed with suits of armour and weapons of war. But in the very depths of the museum was a large room with six sides, and on each wall hung a tapestry of a lady with a unicorn. I was awestruck by their beauty. The six tapestries were made in about 1500 and depict the five senses (taste, hearing, sight, smell, and touch) plus one tapestry called "*À mon seul désir*". My future wife Carmel loved tapestries but had never heard of the Lady and the Unicorn. So when Carmel and I flew from Australia to Paris for a holiday with our four young children, I was able to show Carmel the Lady and the Unicorn tapestries. Carmel had the foresight to bring paper and coloured pencils to occupy the children, who lay on the floor of the gallery drawing while Carmel admired the tapestries. Later still, Carmel and I were able to view the Lady and the Unicorn tapestries again, this time in Sydney when the tapestries were exhibited at the Art Gallery of New South Wales.

I lived in the Cité Universitaire, a hostel for overseas students, in Denfert-Rochereau in the South of Paris. I made a few friends. One of them, a Geordie, never washed his own clothes. He piled them into a cupboard, and took them home for his mother to wash them when he had no more clean clothes. I suppose I must have washed my own clothes. One evening, a kindly Portuguese student put his hand on my thigh and propositioned me. I rebuffed him gently in French. We remained good friends.

I would walk to work each day through the *Parc Montsouris*. Lines of young schoolchildren walked through the park two-by-two in uniform, reminding me strongly of the 1939 children's book *Madeline* by Ludwig Bemelmans. The name Montsouris was originally Moque-Souris, meaning mocks the mice, once a common French name for windmills. There is no longer a windmill in *Parc Montsouris*.

My sister Harriet went on holiday to Bordeaux to improve her schoolgirl French. On the way back she stopped in Paris. I met her at the station. Actually I went to the station two early mornings in a row, because she got the date mixed up. I took her to the house of family friends, the Albis, for dinner. The hostess offered Harriet seconds. "*Non merci, je suis pleine*", said Harriet. Everyone looked shocked. I had to explain to my 15-year-old sister that, although she meant to say: "No thanks, I'm full", she had accidentally said she was pregnant.

Another notable visitor to Paris was my schoolfriend Nigel Calvert (Twiggy). Twiggy came on his motorbike and we visited the Palace at Versailles. He also took a shine to one of the Albis' twin girls, Violette.

Charles Chany was very solicitous. He drove me to the battlefields and cemeteries of the Somme. We wept quietly together at the tragedy of the senseless loss of so many thousands of young lives. My laboratory work included injecting interferon into rabbits to try to get them to produce antiserum (serum containing antibodies). I had no idea how to bleed a rabbit, so Chany said he would show me. The rabbit bit his finger and he swore loudly: "Bazel meg". That was when I learned he was originally Hungarian, and could speak six languages, all with a foreign accent. That was when he learned that I had a Hungarian violin teacher and knew the meaning of his fruity swear-words.

David

In May 1968, there was a famous uprising in Paris, where students occupied universities and joined workers to riot in the streets. They dug up paving stones and threw them at the police. In France the riots were called "*Les événements du mois de Mai*" (the events of the month of May). I started working in Paris in October 1968 and there was still a strong police presence on the streets, often wielding shields. If any youngster with long hair walked close to them they would bang their batons against their shields in unison. The police were a threatening presence and widely hated. At rugby union matches, the massive crowd would chant "CRS – SS", likening the Compagnie Républicaines de Sécurité (police) to the Nazi SS.

I had trouble getting a visa to stay working in France. I had to make six trips to the Préfecture de Police in the city, queuing for well over an hour each time. Whenever I went they asked for a new document. Why they didn't ask for all the documents at once still puzzles me. The French want tourists but they don't really like them. I suspect my visa problems related to the French dislike of foreigners. To keep my sanity, I used to liken the female officers at the Préfecture de Police to the women who knitted at the base of the guillotine. On the sixth visit, the officer said my mother's permission was insufficient; they needed a copy of my father's death certificate, certified by the appropriate authorities. In my best French I said that surely only "*le bon Dieu*" (the good Lord) could certify my father as being dead. I walked back down the queue shedding tears of frustration. Several people waiting in the queue patted my arm sympathetically. I don't think my experience was unique.

After all that, my mother needed an operation. I returned to England to be beside her as she convalesced at a seaside village. That was when I discovered that by going to England, my visa was automatically renewed for six months when I returned to Paris. I need never have gone to the Préfecture de Police at all, but at least I didn't need to go there again.

Friends took me to a concert in an old converted barn. In the middle of the concert, two barn owls flew the length of the hall hooting. It was easy to see why they might have been mistaken for ghosts in olden times.

Towards the end of my time with him, Chany invited me to a virology meeting in the grandiose Royaumont Abbey. He introduced me to an American virologist called Carleton Gajdusek, but cautioned me in French about Gajdusek's predatory nature with boys. Gajdusek was awarded the Nobel Prize for Medicine and Physiology for his work on the transmissibility of the disease kuru. Kuru occurred in the Foré tribe of Papua New Guinea, and was thought to be a genetic disease. However, Gajdusek showed that it was passed on by eating the brains of relatives who had died, and was caused by a "slow virus" or prion. Mad cow disease is another disease caused by prions. Over the years, Gajdusek took more than 50 boys from the Foré tribe back to the United States to live with him and be educated. After one of the boys complained, he was charged with child molestation and imprisoned for a year.

I grew up a lot in those few months in Paris. By the end, my dreams were in French, and when I went to speak English I sometimes used an anglicised version of the French word, e.g. I said "*maintenant*" as main tenant with an English accent when I meant to say "now". I was not completely fluent, but shopkeepers sometimes mistook me for being French. When my mother saw me, she said "You've lost a lot of weight". I had been quite solid when I was playing rugby, so I could do with losing some weight. I was rather proud of my Parisian weight loss.

Stephen was very fluent in Italian by the end of his stay. He could even swear like a Roman taxi-driver (and taught me to do so). He had long curly hair (*capelli lunghi*) and looked like a Botticelli angel. He had travelled to Florence with friends. They all spoke Italian. The meal was excellent and very reasonably priced. The next day Stephen and an American friend went back to the same restaurant, but spoke to each other in English. The bill was five times as much for the same meal. Stephen protested in Italian. "Oh sorry", said the waiter, "we thought you were foreigners, so we gave you the foreigners' price". The waiter took away the bill and came back with a new bill for the same price as the previous day.

Our mother had seen an advertisement in a left-wing journal, *The New Statesman*, for a house rental in Tuscany, and booked it for the summer. Susanna suggested that we all make our way there. Stephen came from Rome, I came from Paris and my mother drove from London with Harriet. The house was near a beautiful little town called Bagni di Lucca (the baths of Lucca, although Lucca was 27 kilometres away). Bagni di Lucca is famous for its hot springs, which were used by the Etruscans, by the Romans and more recently by Napoleon Bonaparte and Lord Byron, among others. On our way into Bagni di Lucca we came across a road called *Viale Evangelina Whipple*, which gave us all the giggles. It turns out that Evangeline Whipple was an American philanthropist and author who moved from the United States to Bagni di Lucca at the end of World War I. She did philanthropic work, including building an orphanage, so the municipality named a street after her.

We drove to the house of the lady who was renting us the house, Mary Iacopucci, to collect the door-keys. Despite her name, Mary was clearly English. Mary and Susanna got talking. Mary had two young children, Dario and Cleo, and was concerned about their schooling. She said she was more particular than most because she went to a very special school. Before Mary said it, I knew what was coming. Mary had been at Dartington Hall School. Her original name was Marion Feld. She was raised in England, travelled to Italy and fell in love with and married Vincenzo Iacopucci. The Italians couldn't manage to say Marion, so she changed her name to Mary.

We had a wonderful holiday in the rented house. We visited the walled city of Barga, and went to a concert there. We drove to Montefegatesi, a beautiful hill-town with a statue of Dante on the top. Susanna thought she could drive up the street, but it was too steep and too narrow. She was stuck, unable to drive up or down. A local man ushered her politely out of the car, jumped in and drove it back down the hill one-handed at a phenomenal speed. We walked in the foothills of the Apennine Mountains. My friend Twiggy had asked if he could join us.

He arrived on his motorcycle with Rosie, the Habs geography mistress, as his pillion passenger. One night when at a concert, Susanna told us she was pretty certain she'd left a boiling pot on the stove and she'd forgotten to switch off the stove. I drove down the steep mountainside rather too fast for comfort, with Twiggy telling me which corners were coming up. His memory was unerring. We found that the stove was indeed still on and that the pot had not boiled dry. We made it back with Twiggy navigating again.

Vincenzo worked for the Department of the Environment. The area around Bagni di Lucca was famed for its chestnut forests, and much of the local industry depended on the chestnut crop, e.g. *marrons glacés*, chestnut flour. Sadly, the chestnut trees had been badly hit by chestnut blight and the industry was in decline. In addition, young villagers were drawn to the cities for adventure. Many houses in the villages surrounding Bagni di Lucca were deserted and starting to deteriorate. Vincenzo decided to buy up some of the abandoned village houses, renovate them in the true Tuscan style, and sell them; this was his way of maintaining the traditional ambience of the area. People in Milan were often interested in buying a house in a village in Tuscany as a country retreat. After our wonderful holiday, so was Susanna. She bought from Vincenzo a disused, renovated 18th century farmhouse in a village called Gombereto, five kilometres from Bagni di Lucca, up a long, winding road. The house had a terrace, originally used to dry chestnuts, but now tiled and commanding a spectacular view of the foothills of the Apennines and of the river valley leading down to Bagni di Lucca.

David in Italy

CHAPTER FIVE: CAMBRIDGE

Clare is a beautiful college, founded in 1326. It has magnificent gardens with some majestic trees which change colour with the seasons. It has an ancient bridge across the river Cam, and is adjacent to the world-famous King's College Chapel. There is a Henry Moore sculpture of *The Fallen Warrior* in one of the courts. At school I had always been near the top of the class, but at Cambridge I was distinctly average, and realised I would need to buckle down to work if I wanted to do well (which I didn't particularly want to do when I started at Clare). David Attenborough was a Fellow of Clare College, but older than us. We never saw him at Clare, although I had heard him give a talk at London Zoo years earlier when I was a teenager.

On our first day at Clare College, aged 18, Stephen and I met our medical tutor, Doctor Wright. All 15 Clare medical students and 3 female students from other colleges were invited to Doc Wright's room. Without a moment's hesitation he went round the room identifying each of us by name, talking about our background and saying what we had been doing in the time between school and university. It was an impressive feat of memory. But we would learn that it would pale into insignificance. When the college was organising a 40 year reunion of its medical students, Doc Wright could reel off all their names straight from his head without a single error. Doc Wright lectured on anatomy, a topic that never excited me, but his lectures were always entertaining. Doc Wright even mentioned Stephen and me in a lecture about the way people use cues: Stephen had long hair, I still had short hair, so you could distinguish us just by our hair, that was his point. Stephen cut his hair short for a show we were in, and suddenly people needed a new cue to distinguish us. The new cue was that Stephen had a very tall girlfriend, and I had a short one (Doc Wright drew these changes with chalk on a blackboard). There were about 200 medical students in our year, attending different colleges. Doc Wright's lecture meant most of them knew of Stephen and me.

One of the physiology lecturers taught us that peristalsis could defy gravity. To prove it, he stood on his head on a table at the front of a large lecture theatre and drank a glass of water upside down, earning a round of applause. We medical students would later repeat this trick when we were in a medical revue, but drinking beer.

We had to dissect a human body as part of our anatomy training. For most of us, it was the first dead body we had ever seen, although the pickled bodies we dissected bore little resemblance to a living being or someone recently deceased. The smell of formalin hung in the air and pricked our eyes. We medical students would talk about and bond over the horrors of dissection. I think most of us learned more about life than about anatomy from dissection.

We worked hard as medical students, certainly a lot harder than students of the humanities. We had some 40 hours a week of lectures, tutorials and dissection. We also had to do a course in pharmacology during the holidays. Although I found anatomy and physiology rather boring and rather removed from clinical medicine, my determination to be a doctor kept me working and I passed the examinations at the end of the first and second years.

However, we medical students were not immune to occasional distractions. A new, innovative, often risqué comedy team of ex-Oxford and Cambridge undergraduates had secured a television contract. They called themselves *Monty Python's Flying Circus.* News of this programme spread in the university and many of us went to Clare Common Room to watch *Monty Python* on a tiny television set. Many were mystified, but a few of us die-hards persisted. Soon there was a tight cohort of students who would gather once a week to giggle at the half-hour programme. We became addicted to sketches such as the Dead Parrot sketch, the cheese shop with no cheese, and the lumberjack song, where one of the butch-looking lumberjacks turned out to prefer picking wildflowers. We idolised the performers, notably John Cleese, Michael Palin and Eric Idle. Eric Idle wrote the irreverent song *Always Look on the Bright Side of Life* which was played during the crucifixion in the Monty Python film *The Life of Brian. Always Look on the Bright Side of Life* became the most popular song to be played in funerals in the United Kingdom. My brother-in-law Anthony Rowlands chose it for the funeral of my sister Harriet.

We Cambridge undergraduates found time to play a lot of sport, and to go to plays and concerts. One November, I got tickets for Steve, Mark Kissin and I to go to the Advent Carol Service in King's College Chapel. The singing of the world famous Kings College choir was exquisite. When we left the Chapel, it was snowing and the ground was covered with a blanket of snow. Men were walking wearing great-coats; women wore muffs. There was no noise, no cars. It could have been a scene from hundreds of years earlier.

I played violin in Clare College Orchestra. The director of music at Clare College was the world famous composer John Rutter. It was wonderful accompanying the celebrated Clare College Choir in Clare College Chapel with John Rutter conducting. My favourite musical memory from those days was driving across the fens to play in a concert with the Clare College Orchestra directed by John Rutter in the majestic Ely Cathedral.

I learned to play bridge at school, but a fellow medical student at Clare College, Richard Butland was a real expert who taught me a huge amount. We played in a regular duplicate tournament in town, and often won. With my brother Stephen and Mark Kissin as second pair, we won the inter-college bridge tournament. Richard, as Captain, and I were first pair for Cambridge University, and we defeated Oxford University in the annual match. Richard got a bit tipsy and was stopped by the police walking along holding a silver trophy and giggling; luckily the police accepted our explanation. Richard and I played for Cambridgeshire in the county championship until we left Cambridge. Richard went on to play for England.

Cambridge University degrees were always three years long (the "tripos"), but the pre-clinical medical course was just two years. Traditionally, students had spent the third year doing research in say physiology or pharmacology, but by our time students had become more adventurous. One of our medical student friends, Roger Kirby, studied Fine Arts in his final year. My brother Stephen and our friend Mark Kissin decided to study Archaeology and Anthropology. Ambitiously, I chose to do a two year Social Anthropology course in one year. I didn't realise then that I was imitating Leonard Elmhirst who had done a four year course in Agriculture in two years at Cornell University.

In our first year at Cambridge we had rooms in Memorial Court, with Henry Moore's sculpture of *The Fallen Warrior* in the garden. In our second year we had to live in the town in unprepossessing accommodation called "digs", which were damp and cold. In our final year, Stephen, Mark Kissin and I did not want to live in digs again and persuaded the powers that be that three of us could share accommodation meant for two. We shared with three others, one of them a future scientist and broadcaster, Jeremy Cherfas, on M staircase; rather pretentiously, we called ourselves the M staircase commune. We would get up at around midday, eat, play competitive sport in the afternoon, have supper, then work until 4am. I suppose it prepared us for being on call as doctors.

I volunteered to work as a carer in a children's home in Cambridge. A girl showed me a calendar she was making. All the months were perfect except December. She had left out December 25th. Foolishly, I pointed out her error. She merely shrugged sadly. Christmas Day had few charms for a girl who lacked a loving family.

David at Clare College, Cambridge

I enjoyed Social Anthropology, although I did have a period of what we called the "existential agonies" (what's the point of it all?) when I thought I would give up my Cambridge degree and go off and do something useful, such as be a social worker. Fortunately, Doc Wright talked some sense into me. I persevered, passed my examinations, and was awarded a BA degree in Social Anthropology. I got a lower second or II-2 degree (known colloquially as a Desmond, after Bishop Tutu).

Cambridge did not have a clinical medical school in our day, so we had to find a medical school. Stephen and I had enjoyed our time together at Clare, but thought it would be better if we went to different London medical schools. Stephen was accepted at King's College Hospital in the south of London, as was a friend from Cambridge, William Tarnow-Mordi. I went to the Middlesex Hospital.

Between finishing at Cambridge and starting at The Middlesex, I had won a scholarship to go to Australia. The scholarship, sponsored by the Australian government and Qantas, was designed to attract university students to visit Australia in the hope of seducing them to come for life. To obtain the scholarship, I needed to arrange work for two months, and was then free to travel for up to a month. Our mother had a friend in Perth, Western Australia, Athol Hockey, who was a paediatrician working with children with disability. Athol and Susanna had trained together in Melbourne. Athol was often referred to as "the mother of medical genetics in Western Australia". I lived with Athol Hockey and her family in her beautiful, historic, jarrah wood house in Peppermint Grove, Perth. Her husband Harold McComb was a plastic surgeon. He used to tutor trainee surgeons in his house. Athol would ask me to take in tea halfway through the tutorial. Harold would do the most beautiful drawings to illustrate the anatomy for his students, like a latter day Leonardo da Vinci. They had four young sons. Two of the sons, David and Robbie, would later form the pop group, The Triffids, who wrote and sang the song *Wide Open Road*. Tragically, Davie would die young due to a cardiac condition resulting from his heroin addiction.

I got up early each morning and took the train into a residential home for children with disability, where I acted as a carer. One day I was taking a boy with autism for a walk, and he refused to walk any further. In frustration I was tugging at his arm, when I caught the disapproving eye of a senior carer. I felt terribly guilty, and resolved in future to treat children with autism as I would want my own child to be treated. It was an important lesson.

One time, Athol McComb drove me to Albany in the south of the state, where the family had a farm. For the entire journey, just over 400 kilometres, both sides of the road were filled with discarded beer bottles and drink cans. I recently journeyed in Western Australia and the roadsides are now pristine. I do not know how the government managed the transformation but it is a considerable achievement.

When my time in Perth was up, I flew to Papua New Guinea, keen to explore this remote country. Port Moresby was unbearably humid; I would be sweating even as I was drying myself after my morning shower. In Moresby, I was invited to lunch by Sir Macfarlane Burnet's son, Ian, who was Head of

Postal Services, and his wife. I hired a car and drove to Goroka in the highlands, with its lush vegetation and much cooler climate. On the way, I stopped and talked to friendly locals, struggling to understand their pidgin English. In Goroka I visited the local hospital which had rudimentary equipment and facilities. I spent my 21st birthday in a car in the Papua New Guinea highlands.

David

CHAPTER SIX: SUSANNA AND LEONARD

Susanna forged a career as a child psychiatrist and as a psychoanalyst. She trained as a senior registrar in child psychiatry under the world-famous child psychiatrist and psychoanalyst Donald Winnicott at Paddington Green, the paediatric wing of St Mary's Hospital, a London teaching hospital. Winnicott did not have children of his own, but he had a remarkable way with children. One day he visited a Norwegian family and spent his time with the children. Afterwards, the children told their parents how well he spoke Norwegian. Winnicott did not know a word of Norwegian, but he understood and could communicate with children. When Winnicott retired, Susanna was appointed as his successor, Physician-in-Charge of the Department of Child Psychiatry at St Mary's. She received a letter from the St Mary's Consultant Committee inviting her to become a member. It was headed "Dear Sir".

Susanna had extraordinary energy. She saw her first psychoanalytic patient from 6.30am every weekday until 7.20am, the psychoanalytic "hour" being 50 minutes long, to allow the analyst time to write notes or go to the toilet between patients. She saw her next psychoanalytic patient from 7.30–8.20am. Then she drove to Paddington Green for a day's work. She saw her final psychoanalytic patient from 6.30–7.20pm. Susanna saw her psychoanalytic patients in a consulting room at our house with a couch for patients, a psychoanalyst's chair and a double door for privacy. Alick, Stephen, Harriet and I timed our movements around the house carefully to avoid meeting Susanna's patients. We succeeded but, when Alick was ill, Susanna used to worry that he might deliberately meet the patients before or after a session. To my knowledge, he never did.

When Alick died, Susanna held the family together while coping with her own grief. Dealing with three teenagers in the aftermath of the loss of her beloved husband cannot have been easy, especially in light of Susanna having "lost" her own father in her early childhood. But somehow we all coped. Stephen and I got almost identical "A" levels despite going to different schools. There's a surprise. Actually our marks were the same in biology and chemistry, but Stephen got one grade better than I did in physics. We were both accepted to study medicine at Clare College, Cambridge. I wish my father had lived long enough to know we had got into Cambridge University.

Steve and I were studying at Cambridge University in 1970 when Leonard Elmhirst started courting our mother. Leonard was happily married to Dorothy Whitney for over 40 years, but she died in 1968. Alick died in 1967. Leonard's wooing of Susanna was very romantic. When he proposed to her, Leonard said "Barkis is willing". This is a jocular reference to Dickens's *David Copperfield*: the stagecoach driver Barkis gets David Copperfield to tell Clara Peggotty that "Barkis is willing", but never proposes directly to her. Since Susanna read Dickens to earn a crust when she was at Bristol, she was well aware of and amused by the reference. Leonard was also genuinely interested in Susanna's children. Leonard was himself a graduate of Cambridge University (Trinity College). He came to visit Stephen and me in Cambridge, and attended a medical revue in which I played Henri Toulouse-Lautrec (on my knees, with shoes tied to the end of my knees and wearing a cloak to hide the rest of my legs). After the performance, Leonard gave me a beautiful book of Toulouse-Lautrec's paintings, which I treasure to this day.

Leonard's Cambridge degree was in history and theology (an "honourable third", the lowest passing degree, he would tell us self-deprecatingly). He originally planned to follow his father into the ministry, but changed his mind. Leonard could bring history to life. He admired Charlemagne as a great leader, and took Susanna to Aix-en-Chapelle to see Charlemagne's grand palace. We went to Florence with Leonard. Leonard took us to see the tiny cell in which the monk Savonarola lived in the 15th century, and the desk at which he worked. Savonarola denounced clerical corruption, despotic rulers and the exploitation of the poor. Then Leonard took us to the Piazza della Signoria and showed us a shiny metal plaque embedded in the cobbled square which commemorated where Savonarola was burned at the stake. In those times, you could pay a heavy price for exposing corruption.

Leonard and Susanna were driving in rural Kent, and a bit unsure if they were on the correct road. They stopped and asked a local man how far it was to their destination. "You're on the right road," he said. It's just three C's from here. Puzzled, Leonard asked him what he meant by three C's. "Arrh, you drive as far as you can see, that's one see, then as far as you can see, that's two sees, then as far as you can see again, and you'll be there."

Leonard was the second of eight consecutive boys born to a Yorkshire curate and his wife. The boys unkindly called their mother "the hardy perennial", because she had a new baby every year. The eighth boy was called Alfred Octavius, as if to say enough is enough. Finally, along came a girl, Irene Rachel, their ninth and last child (although she was always called Iweeny Wachel because that was how her youngest brother pronounced her name).

Leonard was in the army for a year in World War I, but was deemed unfit for military service and was demobilised. He visited India for several months of his own accord. In 1919, he entered Cornell University in Ithaca, New York to study agriculture. He had very little money, but managed to complete a four year course in two years. Leonard was elected President of the Cosmopolitan Club at Cornell, which mostly catered for foreign students. He found it had large debts. In seeking to raise money, Leonard met an heiress Dorothy Straight whom he would marry.

Leonard Elmhirst and Nobel Laureate Rabindranath Tagore

Leonard had clearly made quite a name for himself at Cornell, because Nobel laureate Rabindranath Tagore sought Leonard's help with his local villages in West Bengal which Tagore said were "dying". In 1913, Tagore had received the Nobel Prize for Literature for the English translation *Song Offerings* of his poetry collection *Gitanjali*. Tagore was the first non-European, the first Asian and the only Indian Nobel laureate for literature. In 1921, Leonard travelled to India with Tagore to set up a model rural village and an Institute for Rural Reconstruction (which Tagore later named Sriniketan). When they were building the model village, Leonard saw some men digging latrines. He got a shovel and went to help them. Tagore remonstrated with Leonard that this was work for Untouchables only. Leonard insisted that they needed latrines and he would help. So Tagore got a shovel and joined them.

Leonard later became Tagore's secretary. Between 1923 and 1925, Leonard circumnavigated the globe twice with Tagore. In China, Tagore introduced Leonard to a gardener working in the Royal Palace in Beijing. The gardener was the deposed Emperor. I do not know if Leonard met the Mahatma Gandhi. Gandhi and Tagore were close friends. It was Tagore who gave Gandhi the name Mahatma, meaning "Great Soul" in Sanskrit.

To give an indication of the esteem in which Leonard was held, one day an Indian gentleman came to our house in Hampstead to visit Leonard. When Leonard came down the front garden path to meet him, the gentleman prostrated himself on the ground and kissed Leonard's feet, as Leonard embarrassedly tried to help him up.

Leonard travelled to Tuscany to help Susanna with her newly acquired farmhouse in Gombereto. They named the house Casa Figaro, partly because Susanna was named after Susanna in Mozart's *The Marriage of Figaro*. Leonard found a ruined pigsty with an ancient block of stone marked IHS, which symbolises Jesus Christ. Leonard designed a fireplace with the stone block as the lintel and showed it to Vincenzo. Vincenzo made it happen. Vincenzo adored Leonard, although they lacked a common language. Mary and Vincenzo would take Susanna and Leonard to bijou restaurants in the Tuscan hills. Leonard would tell stories, mostly about his time with Tagore, and Mary would translate them for Vincenzo. One day Vincenzo ordered quail. When the little quail arrived on a platter, Leonard looked so distressed that Vincenzo asked the waiter to take them away.

Vincenzo oversaw the renovations to Casa Figaro himself. One day, he looked at a stone floor that the builder had laid. "Did you lay this floor?", asked Vincenzo. "Yes," the builder said proudly. "Did you use a spirit level?" "Yes". "Well, I think you used your arse instead". And Vincenzo used a spirit level to show him where he would like the floor flatter. There was no malice. Vincenzo and the builder knew each other of old. Vincenzo was just maintaining exacting standards.

We had many wonderful family holidays in Casa Figaro. Indeed, many of our friends from England and Australia have holidayed there for a week or more at a time. One year, a Tasmanian friend, Simon Oakes, and I were clambering up the foothills of the Apennines, when two peregrine falcons flew just over our heads, presumably assessing the danger. Simon became a consultant biochemist at the Royal Children's Hospital in Melbourne, but tragically died of a brain tumour just after getting married, age 39. Some years later, I was walking in the Apennines with my 8-year-old son Mark, when we suddenly came upon a pair of peregrine falcons agitatedly harassing a large bird on the ground. It was a massive golden eagle, presumably trying for their eggs or young.

The toilets at Casa Figaro had no locks, so Susanna said we should all sing when we were in the toilet. However, we did not always remember to warn our friends. One of our friends was sitting on the toilet when Susanna whisked open the door and sprayed him with air freshener.

As Susanna got older and could no longer travel, Stephen, Harriet and I discussed who should take over ownership of Casa Figaro. Harriet and her husband Anthony Rowlands (who later became Mayor of St Albans) were both teachers (Harriet taught English and Drama in Barnet while Anthony taught History at my old school of Haberdashers' Aske's), so were relatively impecunious. I was in Australia. Stephen spoke excellent Italian and could cope with the demands of a house-owner in Italy. So Stephen and his wife Mary, a consultant paediatrician in Ealing, bought the rest of us out, and now own Casa Figaro.

I played rugby union or soccer six days a week for Clare College. One weekend, however, I told my team-mates that I was unavailable. "It had better be a good excuse," they said. "My mother's getting married." Ah. The wedding was in Yorkshire, at the church where Leonard's father had been the pastor. Leonard was 79 years old, Susanna was 51 years old. With his broad Yorkshire accent, the organist said he had never heard of this Purcell feller whose music he had been asked to play (he made it sound like Persil), "but you can't beat your old Buck and Hundle" (Bach and Handel). It was a joyous occasion with a lot of laughter. The weather held out, although the mass outdoor photographs were bracing.

Leonard and Susanna (now Susanna Isaacs-Elmhirst) debated where they would live. If they were to live in England they would likely be torn between competing interests. Leonard's opinion was still in great demand in Dartington. On the other hand, Susanna would be required to be in London for work associated with Paddington Green and for psychoanalytic patients. They toyed with moving to the United States. The great psychoanalyst Wilfred Bion had moved to California; Susanna was tempted to join him. She was invited by Bion to give a talk at the University of Southern California. Shortly before leaving for California, Susanna gave a lecture on child psychiatry to the medical students of St Mary's Hospital, the only lecture they would receive on the topic. The lecture was scheduled for Wednesday afternoon, which was also sports afternoon, a piece of timetabling my mother had never managed to change. St Mary's was big on sport. Only three medical students turned up for her lecture. When she arrived in Los Angeles, Susanna was welcomed by Bion. She gave a talk at the University of Southern California, which was attended by hundreds of keen young attendees who asked intelligent questions.

That was the last straw. Leonard and Susanna moved to Beverly Hills, where they bought a modern bungalow which backed onto woodlands and had a swimming pool in the garden. Leonard loved to swim in the pool. One photo shows him tall and elegant, a towel draped around his neck but not wearing a stitch of clothing. Deer from Beverly Canyon came grazing as far as their back fence. Ruby hummingbirds hovered gracefully as they sucked nectar from the feeders which Susanna and Leonard had hung just outside the house. As a digression, our daughter Anna, like the editor of *The Lancet*, hums all the time when working. Susanna called her her little hummingbird. Anna still wears clothes with hummingbirds on them.

Susanna was appointed Associate Professor at the University of Southern California. She had a consulting room at the front of the house where she saw adult psychoanalytic patients. She also appointed a secretary, Linda, who came from New York with a uniquely New York sense of humour. One day, a patient told Susanna that he had seen a snake outside the consulting room. This was no joking matter, because venomous rattlesnakes inhabited the hillsides of Beverly Hills. Susanna asked Linda to buy her a snake book. "So what are you gonna do now? Teach it to read?", asked Linda. We all loved Linda.

Shortly before leaving England it was discovered at a routine medical examination that Leonard had a large, asymptomatic abdominal aortic aneurysm. Leonard could bleed to death if the aneurysm ruptured spontaneously, but an elective operation was not without risk. Leonard saw a London surgeon who recommended an elective operation, but the surgeon had no bedside manner and Leonard didn't warm to him. He asked around for a second opinion and went to see a lovely Scottish surgeon, who explained the risks and benefits of an elective operation. After this, Leonard decided against the operation. It was a sad irony that Susanna was again married to a man with abnormal blood vessels and a Sword of Damocles hanging over his head.

Leonard and Susanna were idyllically happy in Beverly Hills. We children visited them there, shared in their happiness and went to see something of Los Angeles. I remember going to the suburb of Watts, which would later be the site of vicious race riots. We went to see Watts Towers, which were high tapering towers built in his backyard by a poor Italian migrant using only rubbish, including broken glass and lids of Coca cola bottles.

After Alick's debilitating illness, 51-year-old Susanna was unable to face looking after an incapacitated Leonard, about to enter his eighties, which was a possible complication of a bleed. Leonard and Susanna agreed that if Leonard bled from his aneurysm, Susanna would treat him at home. Tragically, Leonard and Susanna only had a year of life together in Beverly Hills before Leonard bled from his aneurysm. Susanna treated Leonard with morphine for pain relief, and he died in her arms. I have always wondered if Leonard might not have had several more happy years if he had been operated on to stop the bleeding. On the other hand, Leonard had made the decision and who else should make a decision about their own mortality? I found it hard to cry when my father died, but I wept copious tears when I received a phone call from Susanna telling me of Leonard's death. Poor Susanna had to bury two of the 20th century's outstanding men.

Carmel and I named our eldest son Benjamin Leonard in honour of Leonard Elmhirst (my sister Harriet had already named her first-born daughter Alice in memory of Alick and my brother would later name his only son Jonathan Bernard Alick after both his grandparents).

Susanna stayed in her Beverly Hills home for five more years. What brought her back to her Hampstead house was the arrival of her first grandchild, our daughter Anna. Susanna was a thoughtful, generous grandmother. Her house was full of children's toys and videotapes of children's films like *Mary Poppins* and *Bedknobs and Broomsticks*, which the grandchildren would watch snuggled up in her bed with their grandmother. She was ultra-indulgent and let them put as many lumps of sugar as they wanted into their orange juice or hot chocolate. Susanna took all the grandchildren to a show every Christmas. Depending what was on it might be a ballet like *The Nutcracker Suite*, a short play like Dickens's *A Christmas Carol*, or a musical like *Jesus Christ Superstar* or *Billy Elliot*.

Susanna had a stubborn tendency to favour her granddaughters over her grandsons, which sometimes caused ructions with me. One time, she took her two granddaughters and her two grandsons shopping and bought shoes for the girls, but not the boys. I confronted her about it and she called me an f...ing ungrateful wretch. I think her favouritism had something to do with being abandoned by her father as a young child, but I was amazed that a psychoanalyst would deny this favouritism despite being presented (by me) with incontrovertible evidence. Psychiatrists and psychoanalysts are not immune from bias and lack of insight.

Tagore visiting the Forbidden City in Beijing in May 1924
Leonard Elmhirst, Tagore's secretary, is in the centre at the back

Back in London, Susanna was appointed as consultant psychiatrist to the Coram Adoption Service, where she remained from 1988–1996. Thomas Coram was a 19th century sea captain and philanthropist. Shocked to see destitute and dying children on the streets of London, Coram established the Foundling Hospital in 1839, near the site of Great Ormond Street Hospital, which was opened just 13 years later. George Frederick Handel was a supporter of Thomas Coram. Susanna took me to a concert in the Coram Centre, where there were several musical instruments dating from Handel's time. The book *Coram Boy* by Jamila Gavin was adapted into a powerful play by Helen Edmundson, which we saw with Susanna. When Susanna died, Jeanne Kaniuk of the Coram Adoption Service wrote to *The Guardian* newspaper: "She understood troubled children and conveyed hopefulness for their ability to heal and grow. The organisation's social workers appreciated not only the way she helped us to understand the children and to provide support for them and their families, but also the generosity of spirit she showed. Sue was always interested in our ideas, and enabled us all to absorb new ideas and to change our practice without fear of criticism or failure. She was a kind-hearted teacher who had an ongoing influence on us."

In her late seventies, Susanna suffered a stroke and was forced to give up working. My sister Harriet, her husband Anthony and children Alice and Sam lived in the old Roman town of St Albans. They moved into a much larger house and built a "granny flat" for Susanna that would give her privacy and proximity. The granny flat was still under construction, so my wife Carmel and I had Susanna stay with us in Sydney for three months. The old enmities about Carmel and I leaving England were long since forgiven. After three months, Susanna returned to England and moved into the St Albans house. Susanna was happiest when Alice or Sam came to visit her. She had a carer who adored her and was very solicitous. Stephen's eldest daughter Catherine married Tom

W. in January 2010. It was bitterly cold. Susanna insisted on attending the wedding. Carmel and I and our children flew out from Australia for it. Whether or not it had anything to do with the cold, Susanna deteriorated after the wedding. Carmel and I had only arrived back in Sydney two days earlier when we heard that Susanna had died at the age of 88. We turned round and flew back. I gave the eulogy at the funeral. I had thought long and hard what to say and gave the eulogy without stumbling. But when I sat down on the pew next to Carmel, I burst into floods of tears. I hadn't seen that coming at all. Les Brent, who attended the funeral, told me he had not known a lot of what I said about Susanna. He used my notes to write an obituary, which was published in *The Guardian* newspaper.

Susanna Isaacs-Elmhirst

CHAPTER SEVEN: MEDICAL STUDENT LIFE

The Middlesex Hospital, which sadly no longer exists, was in the vibrant West End of London. This is where I was introduced to clinical medicine, to seeing patients on the ward, and I loved it. The first ward round I attended, I wore a purple hat and similarly colourful clothes, but I soon learned that what I considered rather flash at Cambridge was frowned upon in a London medical school. I did have a mild run-in with a respiratory consultant regarding a 40-year-old woman with young children who had lung cancer. The consultant told us he was going to tell her she had a growth. I asked what he would say if she asked if she had cancer. He said he would say it was a tumour. I thought this was tantamount to lying to her, and that we had a duty to tell her the truth, and allow her to arrange her affairs. By then I had learned to be somewhat subtle when I challenged a consultant and I did not push my point too hard. His rationale was presumably "not to worry" the patient. In those days it was common to deceive patients to save them from worrying unduly. I feel time has justified my feeling that it was better to be truthful so that patients could plan the end of their lives: modern practice in cancer management emphasises the importance of truth-telling.

We were a very close-knit group of medical students at The Middlesex Hospital. Jennifer Patterson (now Lady Jennifer Stringer, wife of Sir Howard Stringer, the first non-Japanese Chief Executive Officer of Sony) who would become a dermatologist and David Redman (consultant anaesthetist) had done their pre-clinical medical studies at The Middlesex Hospital. Tony Delamothe came originally from Bowen in Far North Queensland, did his pre-clinical years in Brisbane, but moved to London with his family when his doctor–politician father was appointed to a post in London. Stephen and I drove Tony to Cambridge to hear Lou Reed, singer and guitarist in the alternative rock band, *The Velvet Underground*, which was managed by Andy Warhol. The concert was in the incongruous venue of a Cambridge University lecture theatre, but it was a triumph. I had never heard of Lou Reed, but when he played *Walk on the Wild* Side, I was a fan for life. That night we all slept on the floor of a friend from our Cambridge undergraduate days. It was the start of a lifelong friendship. Tony did a doctorate in endocrinology, but then switched to journalism and became deputy editor at the British Medical Journal (BMJ). Mick Powell had trained as an undergraduate in Oxford. He became a famous neurosurgeon at Queen's Square in London. My daughter Anna did a brief sojourn with Mick when she was a medical student, and said he was lovely to everyone, no matter their status, and he was very kind to women. All those qualities were rare in neurosurgeons in those days. Nick Boon who became a top Edinburgh-based cardiologist, Jeremy Gibbs (consultant neurologist), Roger Kirby (urologist, fundraiser and President of the Royal Society of Medicine), Mark Kissin (breast cancer and melanoma surgeon) and Norman Peden (Dundee-based endocrinologist who married paediatrician Aline Russell, a Middlesex Hospital undergraduate) had all done their pre-clinical training at Cambridge University. We studied together, played poker together (for pennies), went on holiday together, and laughed a lot together. Mark Kissin participated in the medical revue in his first year at The Middlesex Hospital, then was asked to be Director next year. Mark, Stephen and I wrote the script in its entirety. Mark called the revue *Last Plaster in Paris.* Henri Toulouse-Lautrec was born again and I played him again. All the actors in the revue studied or worked at the Middlesex Hospital. Many became my lifelong friends: Judith Scallan (Jude), who married Jeremy Gibbs. Annie Pensabene, who married Mark Kissin's cousin Brian Aarons. Brian died tragically young from a brain tumour. Jennifer Patterson, Mick Powell and David Redman (Rosco) were also in the cast, and remain lifelong friends, even 35 years after Carmel and I left for Australia. *Last Plaster in Paris* played for ten nights, at the end of which we were all exhausted and in need of detoxification.

Later, Mark Kissin was invited to perform a cabaret for the annual May Ball at Clare College, Cambridge. He recruited me, my brother Stephen, a Middlesex Hospital undergraduate Tony Costello (who later became Professor of Global Health at University College London) and Jenny Riches, a Middlesex Hospital physiotherapist, to perform with him. Mark, Stephen and I wrote sketches for the performance, Tony had a hilarious magic routine, and I wrote a song entitled "I always seem to spend my time under graduates" which Jenny sang while I accompanied her on the violin. The ball went on all night and we did three performances which were packed out and cheered by drunken revellers. It was a wonderfully debauched night. Only the audience was debauched and drunk. Sadly, the performers felt we needed to remain sober in order to perform well.

Once a week, a group of us medical students walked to the specialist hospital at Queen Square for tutorials on neurology and neurosurgery. Tony Delamothe encouraged us to visit the British Museum on the way back to the Middlesex. Those of us who joined him would visit a different room each week. Our Australian friend was far more cultured than any of the rest of us medical students.

We had occasional gynaecology tutorials at a hospital in Soho. The Queen's gynaecologist had a group of us medical students gather at the foot of a woman's bed. Without warning, he pulled back the bedsheet, revealing the woman's ulcerated uterus prolapsed between her legs. He intended to shock us. He certainly succeeded, but only because we were horrified that a doctor could betray a patient's trust and dignity so callously. How ironic that the Queen's gynaecologist was such a misogynist.

Shortly before we finished at The Middlesex Hospital, we had an elective period where we could study anywhere in the world if we could arrange it and pay for it. Previous elective students had recorded their experiences in a book. I wanted to go to Africa. I talked to one student who had gone where I wanted to go. He had camped near the famous Ngorongoro Crater. He woke in the night to a Masai spear at his throat. His assailants took everything he had, including passport and money, but not his life. Only slightly deterred, I arranged to do my elective at Kilimanjaro Christian Medical Centre (KCMC), at the foot of Mount Kilimanjaro in Tanzania. Roger Kirby, meanwhile, arranged to go to a mission hospital in Meru, Kenya. We agreed to meet up at Meru to travel for a couple of weeks when we had completed our electives.

I flew to the Tanzanian capital, Dar es Salaam, and took buses to Mount Kilimanjaro. As we approached the mountain there were great plains dotted with flat-topped acacia trees. Statuesque giraffe looked up as we passed. The mountain soars majestically up from the plains. When it is snow-topped it is reminiscent of Mount Fuji.

At KCMC, I learned to do lumbar punctures on children with suspected meningitis, but using a plain needle because the hospital could not afford the bevelled, double-barrelled lumbar puncture needles used in Western countries. The sinks on the wards did not work, so the consultant, a formally dressed Englishman, would rinse his hands in a bowl of soapy water attached to the trolley full of patients' notes that he pushed around the ward. Then he would dry his hands on a towel hanging from the trolley.

I saw young children die from measles and infants die from neonatal tetanus. The experience at KCMC was sobering, but it convinced me of the importance of childhood immunisation, convinced me to do paediatrics, and stirred an ambition to do paediatric infectious diseases.

One weekend, I caught buses to the Serengeti National Park. There was a swanky Tourist Lodge at the Park, but I couldn't possibly afford it. With the optimism of youth, I thought something would come up, and it did. On the bus

I started chatting to a young African man. He told me he worked at the Lodge and could put me up. He lived in a bare hut with few facilities, and no electricity. He let me sleep on the floor. I had also met a Norwegian family who were camping at the campsite a mile from the Lodge. They had no room in their tent, but said they would drive me round the Serengeti if I met them at their tent in the morning.

On the equator, the sun rises suddenly and sets suddenly with very little warning. I woke in the hut in complete blackness. After a few minutes there was a sudden glow of light. I got up, thanked my host and walked along the track towards the campsite. The sun was just showing over the horizon. Everything was suffused with a pink glow. I passed a herd of zebra and they were pink and black. The walk to the campsite took longer than I had expected. I began to think of lions returning from an unsuccessful night's hunting. Perhaps I could climb an acacia tree. Damn. The lions in the Serengeti were notoriously good tree climbers. If hungry lions came along I was a goner, I decided. But what about buffalo? Some of the nastiest injuries I had witnessed at KCMC were farmers who had been gored in the abdomen by buffalo. Buffalo can't climb trees. As I walked, I kept an eye out for the nearest tree. I turned a corner and found myself face to face with a large buffalo wallowing in a waterhole. I turned and started to run towards the tree, my heart thumping. I looked over my shoulder and saw that there were half a dozen buffalo in the waterhole, but they were all lumbering away from me in the opposite direction. I resumed walking along the track, only slightly hysterical. The campsite was round the next corner. I heaved a huge sigh of relief. I didn't tell the Norwegian family about my adventure, probably the most foolhardy thing I ever did.

I had a wonderful time with the Norwegian family. A ranger alerted us to a leopard lying along the branch of a tree, its tail hanging down. We saw a pack of Cape hunting dogs. We saw tall secretary birds, so-called because their crest looks like a quill behind a secretary's ear. These birds kick venomous snakes lurking in the long grass, to kill and eat them. We saw majestic East African cranes with their golden crest and red throats. We visited the Ngorongoro Crater, where all the animals seemed to be squeezed together and to show no fear of humans.

When I had finished my elective at KCMC, I took buses to Meru in Kenya to meet Roger Kirby. Friends of Roger's drove us to the panoramic Great Rift Valley, then on to dazzling blue Lake Naivasha, where literally thousands of statuesque pink flamingos strutted in unison. Roger and I climbed Mount Kenya with two of his friends. I had not climbed Mount Kilimanjaro because it was a 5-day climb and I lacked the time. However, at KCMC, I saw lots of young men and women with pulmonary oedema from altitude sickness. Older people never seemed to get so sick, perhaps because they climbed slower and adapted better. One of Roger's friends brought a huge supply of lemon curd sandwiches. The others had altitude sickness and their appetites suffered, but I had no such problem and hoed into the sandwiches. I have no idea why he chose lemon curd.

Later, Roger and I travelled to the Masai Mara and camped there. We cooked outside our tent. It rained and we left our cooking utensils outside for the rain to clean them. In the night, we were woken by crunching noises, but didn't dare look outside. In the morning, we found that our kettle had been gnawed and we saw a pair of hyenas nearby watching us.

Roger and I travelled up the Kenyan coast to the ancient coastal city of Mombasa, founded in 900 AD. The streets of Mombasa could have been there for centuries. One shop stocked row after row of ancient bottles of perfume. We wondered if any contained ambergris, given that Mombasa would have traded with whalers. We took a small boat out to one of the dhows moored offshore, which had a beautiful curved sail. Dhows are trading vessels, which are thought to have originated in India some time between 600 BC and 600 AD. On the wooden deck of the dhow in Mombasa was a huge wicker basket full of oranges, to prevent scurvy presumably. Men in traditional Arab clothes sat around smoking hookahs.

There was nothing to suggest the dhow had not been there for hundreds of years.

Roger and I carried on up the coast to the coastal town of Malindi, where we stayed with two female acquaintances, one of whom was a marine photographer. They took us out on their boat from where we snorkelled. A massive shoal of silver barracuda swam close by, perhaps too close in view of their razor-sharp teeth, although the photographer assured us we were in no danger. Suddenly, a white-haired figure surfaced out of the vast, empty expanse of ocean. It was Jon Pertwee, the actor who played Doctor Who. Malindi was known to attract celebrities, but we were speechless, half expecting the Tardis to surface beside him.

Roger had to return to England, but I continued heading north towards Lamu by bus. At one point something under the bus started making a grinding noise. The driver, sighed, stopped the bus, found a rock, slid under the bus and started hitting the underneath with the rock. After a bit, he re-emerged satisfied, restarted the bus and we continued without the grinding noise. We reached the Tana River, a wide river where crocodiles are known to claim the lives of children every year. There was a wooden bridge, but only on one side of the river and only the length of a bus. We passengers were all told to get out of the bus. The driver drove the bus onto the bridge. The passengers were all told to grab hold of ropes that were going through loops on the bridge and across the river. Then we passengers all pulled the bus and the floating bridge slowly crossed the river. It was a novel way to cross a crocodile-infested river.

I stayed overnight at a mission hospital. Most of the patients had schistosomiasis of the bladder. Schistosomiasis, sometimes called bilharzia, is a parasitic worm infestation transmitted by freshwater snails. Humans are infected by swimming in or even walking barefoot in an infected lake. The worms can then find their way through the bloodstream to the bladder. I went for a late afternoon walk to the nearby lake. As I walked, my footsteps made a crunching sound. I looked down and found the ground was covered with the shells of dead snails. Luckily I was wearing shoes, not sandals. As I neared the lake, the sun was setting fiery red. On a small boat, two men were silhouetted as they threw out their fishing nets. All around them the heads of hippopotamus rose and sank in the rose-tinged water.

The bus reached the magical island of Lamu, just off the Kenyan coast. The Swahili settlement of Lamu Island dates from the 12th century. There are no cars on the island, which features long deserted beaches and ancient houses. Lamu was my last stop in Africa and felt like something of a dream.

I returned to the reality of final examinations, which were held at Cambridge. Despite me getting quite anxious about the exams, we all passed. We were MBBChir (Bachelor of Medicine, Bachelor of Surgery).

David on the Thames, 1978

CHAPTER EIGHT: EARLY MEDICAL YEARS

Our "houseman year" consisted of six months of medicine and six months of surgery.

I started with surgery: I had a position as house surgeon at the Central Middlesex Hospital in Acton, West London doing general and vascular surgery. As a last act of defiant independence before becoming regularly employed for life, I went to a party. The party was on a Wednesday and I stayed until midnight. The next morning I turned up at work to find I would not be off duty until the next Tuesday. Our team operated and was on call for admissions every Monday and Thursday. In addition we were on from Friday to Sunday every fourth weekend. It just so happened that we were entering one of those weekends. I have no memory whether I brought sufficient underwear and shirts to last me for six days in a row.

The consultant and the registrar did all the operations. My job was to clerk all the patients, diagnose what was wrong with them and assist the surgeon by holding retractors during the operations. The vascular operations could go for as long as six hours. I got an average of two hours sleep a night for my first five nights. I drove home on Tuesday lunchtime, and was stopped by the police for erratic driving. When I proved to them that I was a doctor and my poor driving was from lack of sleep not excess of any illicit substance, they sent me off with a cheery: "Drive safely, Doc."

We worked very hard but partied hard, too. One weekend when I wasn't working I went to a party at The Middlesex Hospital. I had imbibed a fair amount and Roger Kirby dunked me in a bath full of water. I fell, cut my head on a wall, and had to attend the Emergency Department at the hospital. A nurse who had been in the Middlesex Revue with us, Annie Pensabene (which translates as "*think well*"), stitched my head and found a leaf spine that had broken off and been embedded there from when I was walking in a rainforest in Meru, Kenya with Roger Kirby. I was admitted to The Middlesex Hospital for observation as a head injury, one of several that night. On the ward round the next morning, the registrar described the patients with head injuries to the consultant, who asked each time whether there was a history of alcohol intake. When the round reached me, the registrar said: "One of our ex-medical students with a head injury". I said: "Strongly positive alcoholic history, sir". The consultant said: "Oh, jolly bad luck", and patted my leg kindly. I was allowed home when my clothes had dried.

One day the surgical registrar was ill and went off to bed. A 9-year-old boy came to the Emergency Department with abdominal pain and I diagnosed appendicitis. I rang the registrar to operate, but he groaned and said: "I'm too sick. You do it. You've seen me do them before." See one, do one, teach one. I was very uncertain of myself, but I had little choice. I took the child to theatre. I remember having loops of bowel tucked under my arm as I searched for the appendix. A canny scrub nurse pointed towards the appendix. The appendix was inflamed and I succeeded in taking it out and sewing up the child's abdomen. I completed the operation in 45 minutes, when the registrar usually took 15 minutes. My travails with the boy's appendix remind me of Mikhail Bulgakov's book *A Young Doctor's Notebook*, in which he describes working alone as a newly qualified doctor in remote country Russia and muddling through operations with the help of a textbook and a good nurse. I watched my child patient afterwards with an eagle eye, but thankfully he made a complete and uncomplicated recovery. If I was his parent, I would have been very unhappy that his appendectomy was entrusted to a very junior doctor doing the operation for the very first time and unsupervised.

Another day, a young East African mother of 3 young children presented to the Central Middlesex Hospital with a painful abscess at the base of her spine, a so-called pilonidal abscess. I clerked her and her clinical examination was completely normal. For the operation to drain the abscess, the young anaesthetist intubated her (put a breathing tube down), and the surgical registrar then turned the patient onto her front to expose the abscess. The registrar had a medical student do the operation under his supervision, which slowed the operation. It was in the days before we had pulse oximeters to check that patients were adequately oxygenated. The patient was very dark-skinned, which meant it was hard to tell whether or not she was cyanosed (blue through lack of oxygen). At one point during the operation, the anaesthetist looked a bit concerned, but he felt the patient's pulse and nodded reassuringly. When the operation ended, however, the patient had no pulse and we started chest compression. A senior consultant surgeon came in from next door, looked in the patient's mouth and said, very softly: "The tube's down the oesophagus." He whipped it out and re-inserted it down the trachea. Either the tube had been down the oesophagus (food-pipe) instead of the trachea (wind-pipe) throughout the operation or it had been dislodged when the patient was turned over. We were unable to resuscitate the poor woman. The registrar and I had to break the news to her husband. He broke down and berated himself for not bringing her to hospital sooner. Afterwards I asked the registrar why he had not mentioned the possible anaesthetic mishap. He told me I would ruin my own career as well as that of the anaesthetic registrar if I told the husband. I talked to the anaesthetic consultant and he said he couldn't be sure the tube was wrongly placed. I talked to my surgical consultant and he was sympathetic but said that, without the support of the anaesthetic consultant, I risked my career if I blew the whistle. The autopsy found that the patient had endomyocardial fibrosis, a heart condition known to occur in East Africa, and her death was attributed to that, rightly or wrongly.

Years later, a young consultant anaesthetist Stephen Bolsin became concerned. In Bristol, where he worked, children needing paediatric heart surgery were transferred to London for surgery. This was costly for the local health authority, which decided to start doing the operations in Bristol. However, the Bristol cardiac surgeon had no experience with children and the mortality of his paediatric heart operations was considerably higher than that in major paediatric centres like Great Ormond Street. Stephen Bolsin pointed out the high mortality. Instead of praising Dr Bolsin and addressing the high mortality, the local health authority pilloried him and accused him of undermining the cardiac surgical team. Stephen Bolsin persisted and eventually Bristol was forced to employ paediatric cardiac surgeons. But Stephen Bolsin was branded a trouble-maker and was unable to get employment anywhere in the United Kingdom. He and his family left England and moved to Geelong near Melbourne, where he was recognised as a brave whistle-blower who had saved children's lives. Stephen Bolsin has my unbridled admiration. But he paid a high price for being a whistle-blower. People who are considering blowing the whistle should take into account the possible deleterious effect that being a whistle-blower may have on one's career and on one's family. They may still decide to blow the whistle, like brave Stephen Bolsin, but they should have considered the probable adverse effects of doing so first.

Nobody taught me to convey bad news. I observed my registrar doing it and thought about what he did well and what he might have done better. We were given a lot of responsibility as junior doctors doing our first six months. One day I was left to impart the news that our operation on a man who was vomiting showed he had inoperable stomach cancer. I found the man on the ward, awake and surrounded by his family. I thought they all ought to know. I pulled the curtains round the bed for some pretence of privacy, and told the whole family the diagnosis and the poor prognosis. I answered their questions as best I could. I walked back down the ward with tears in my eyes, and a patient said: "It can be tough, can't it, Doc?" I survived rather than enjoyed my surgical six months.

Acton was Dickensian. The hospital was next to the Guinness factory; the area was grimy and polluted. After six months, I craved fresh air. I heard about an excellent job in Poole, Dorset, applied and was successful. I was a houseman in general medicine and oncology. Poole Hospital was several storeys high. The doctors' rooms were on the top floor. Initially I faced the town, but after a month I was moved to a room overlooking Poole Harbour. The harbour is a drowned valley formed at the end of the last Ice Age. It was a long, hot summer. I always left my curtains open, so that I would be woken by the sun as it rose over the harbour. It was a sight of which I never tired.

When I arrived, I found that I had 51 patients under my care. But I never felt flustered. The consultant, whom I admired, said I had to find one or two words, no more, which summed up each of his patients, so that when we did a ward round he could easily remember them. It was like a game, but it helped shorten ward rounds, so it had value.

I enjoyed oncology and even toyed with the idea of doing paediatric oncology, but I found the grief of losing so many patients too overwhelming. One day, we were subjected to a routine inspection of the oncology facilities. When the inspectors came to a locked cupboard and asked what was in it, I thought I saw the senior nurse wince before she said "Drugs". The inspectors asked her to open the cupboard. It was full of bottles of whisky and gin. Everyone laughed.

Very early one morning I was woken by the emergency bleep I carried, which alerted me that there was a patient in the emergency department who had suffered a cardiac arrest. I leapt out of bed and rushed to the emergency department in my pyjamas. A young man was being wheeled past on a trolley. I felt for his femoral pulses and could not feel them. I thumped him on the chest to get his heart beating, preparatory to commencing cardiopulmonary resuscitation. The man sat up, groaned and said: "Don't do that, please, Doc.

I only fainted". There was a general tittering and I slunk off shamefacedly to get dressed.

We worked hard but the hospital was well staffed so, when we had worked overnight, we got a day off. I fell in love with Dorset, which is a beautiful county. Dorset is Thomas Hardy country. One weekend, some of my Middlesex Hospital medical student friends and their partners came down for the weekend. We visited Lulworth Cove, which was a smugglers' haunt. We visited the atmospheric ruin of Corfe Castle. We even saw a snake swimming across a river. I was very happy at Poole.

When I finished my house jobs I found it impossible to get a paediatric job. The paediatric departments all wanted me to do a year of general medicine first and to pass the first written part of the examination for the Royal College of Physicians, which was the same examination for adult and paediatric candidates (the Member of the Royal College of Physicians or MRCP exam). So I found myself a Senior House Officer (SHO) position in general and respiratory medicine in Exeter, on the edge of Dartmoor. I was in Devon and liked the solitude of the moors. Dartington was not far away. The hospital was an isolated place with few distractions and I was able to work for and pass the MRCP written examination. I also attended a course in Plymouth preparing doctors for the clinical examination.

One day in Exeter, the consultant admitted a 19-year-old man who had cystic fibrosis. His lung function had deteriorated and the consultant brought him in for a "tune-up", which involved giving the patient antibiotics and physiotherapy, usually for two weeks. Something was clearly troubling the young man, so I talked to him and asked what was the matter. He was a bit coy, so I asked him if he was worried about sex. He nodded. "Oh I see", I said. "You have heard that men with cystic fibrosis may have problems with sex. Don't worry. You can have sex OK. You might have problems getting someone pregnant. But at your age, that's probably an advantage." The next day, the consultant asked me what I had done to make the young man so much better already, when a tune-up usually took two weeks. I shrugged and denied any knowledge of the cause of the young man's improvement.

I always feared unemployment. I was due to be unemployed for three weeks at the end of my Exeter job. I did a general practitioner (GP) locum in Exeter for a week. One evening I was called to see a woman with abdominal pain. As I arrived, my little Mini developed a flat tyre. The woman had extremely painful biliary colic due to a stone in her bile duct. At my request, her husband changed my tyre while I gave his wife morphine, then drove her to hospital on the new tyre.

Another evening, I was asked to see a man with chest pain. I expected an elderly man with a heart attack, but when I arrived, it was a 19-year-old in great pain from a pneumothorax (air between the lung and the chest wall). The pneumothorax needed draining in hospital, but as a temporising measure, I popped a green needle into his chest. The air came out with a hiss and he breathed a sigh of relief as the pain eased. But after a while the needle blocked, so I inserted another one and called an ambulance. As we sat in the ambulance, I kept inserting more and more needles. When we arrived at the hospital, the registrar and erstwhile colleague asked if I had been trying to cure the young man with acupuncture. The registrar kindly allowed me to insert the definitive chest drain which would remain in place for a few days until the lung was fully re-expanded and the leak sealed. The other GP's were amazed at how I seemed to attract patients with rare conditions they hardly ever saw.

CHAPTER NINE: PAEDIATRIC TRAINING AND MARRIAGE

With an extra year of medical training and my written MRCP examination, I was able to apply successfully for an SHO position in paediatrics at Northwick Park Hospital in Harrow, Middlesex on the outskirts of London. I immediately knew that paediatrics was my true vocation. Paediatricians had none of the pomposity so common in adult physicians and surgeons, perhaps because children lack artifice. Our consultants expected us to call them by their first names. Their names were Bernard (Bernie) Valman and Mike Liberman. Amongst ourselves we jokingly referred to them as Valium and Librium. Indeed, we put on a short revue at Northwick Park and wrote a song called *The Valium and Librium Blues* for it. Bernie and Mike were kind, approachable people. When I started, Mike Levin was finishing his SHO year. He would become a firm friend and one of the leading paediatric infectious disease specialists in the world, working mainly on meningococcal infections and Kawasaki disease. He is now Professor of Paediatrics and International Child Health at Imperial College, London. Barbara Ansell, the "Queen of childhood arthritis", worked at Northwick Park Hospital, and I had the pleasure of looking after her patients if they were admitted to hospital. Mary Cummins was the experienced senior registrar.

I loved Bernie and Mike, and learned a lot from them, from Barbara Ansell, from Mary Cummins and from Mike Levin, although I never totally overcame my fear of intubating tiny babies. While I was at Northwick Park, I passed the adult clinical examination of the Royal College of Physicians to become MRCP. I toyed with doing the paediatric clinical, but I had trained for the adult exam in Plymouth and wanted the exam out of the way. I was now a Member of the Royal College of Physicians (MRCP). I would have had the same letters if I had sat the paediatric clinical examination.

I worked as a junior doctor in a "day unit", where children came for investigations or treatment. One little boy needed to come for blood tests, each week for many weeks. Every week he screamed and thrashed and kicked the nurse who tried to hold him still, as I made a mess of trying to take his blood. One day I asked him: "Henry. When do you think you will stop kicking the nurse when I take your blood?" "When I'm five." "But that's next week", I said. "Yes" he said. The next week, Henry held out his arm to have his blood taken and made absolutely no fuss. Nor did he for the remaining weeks he came to me to take his blood. I had inadvertently discovered the importance of giving very young children choice, not only in medicine but in life generally.

I never did manage to take blood or put up drips well. When I worked as a registrar in Sydney, I regularly had to call a fellow registrar for help because I had missed so many times. It was a great relief for me, and more so for the patients, when I became senior enough to delegate the taking of blood.

By now I had met the love of my life. In a book I wrote, I called Carmel the lodestone of my existence, which is an oblique reference to Rabindranath Tagore who wrote a Fantasy called *The Lodestone*. Carmel Foster was born in Canberra, one of eight children. She is Catholic, as is my twin brother Stephen's wife, Mary Cummins. Is that the concordance of identical twins or did it have something unconscious to do with our mother being strongly anti-Catholic? Carmel trained as a nurse at Canberra Hospital. Then, determined to see the world, she flew to Bali, Djakarta, Singapore and Bangkok, each for a couple of days, before flying to Kathmandu and joining an organised bus tour. She loved the ruins in Persepolis and had many adventures on the way to London. We met at a party in Oxford being given by mutual friends. I was enchanted by this resourceful young woman. It helped that she was beautiful, with a winning smile and a sharp sense of humour. She also had wonderful red hair. Was it a coincidence that she is Australian or was that part of her attraction?

"Looks cheap to feed," George Foster.
Carmel and David, Hollycroft, 1978

Although we met in Oxford, we were both living in London. Oxford would figure large in our lives later, and of course I had been conceived in Australia, had visited there aged 21, and had a lifelong fascination with Australia. Carmel and I started dating. At Northwick Park Hospital, the junior doctors were given two holidays a year of one month each, but we were told when to take them. This helped with rostering. Carmel and I had a month to spend together. For two weeks, I drove Carmel to various places she wanted to see, including the ancient cathedral at Tunbridge Wells and Hadrian's Wall, which was cold and misty but, we reassured ourselves, how the Romans would have seen it most of the time. We drove up to Scotland and stayed with Norman and Aline Peden, who took us to visit an iron age fort on Dunsinane Hill (think Macbeth). For the second fortnight, we took a fly–drive holiday to Morocco, landing in Tangiers, collecting a hire car and heading south. We crossed the Atlas Mountains and drove down to Marrakesh, via the colourful town of Fez. It was my first time in North Africa and it was very different from East Africa. But my French came in useful and we travelled safely, without hindrance and had a great trip. Carmel said that she was pleased to have my company, because when she travelled on her own, men were all over her like a rash.

Soon after, we were engaged, although I am embarrassed to say I proposed sitting in my car in the family garage, which was a decidedly unromantic setting. Carmel sent a photo of us to her parents, me with long hair and wearing a kaftan I bought in Morocco. Her father's summary of his prospective son-in-law was: "Looks cheap to feed". I could see where Carmel got her sense of humour from.

In 1978, Steve and his girlfriend Liz, Carmel and I drove to a disused military airport Blackbushe Aerodrome in Surrey for a rock concert. We heard Joan Armatrading and Eric Clapton. The finale was Bob Dylan. A crowd of 250,000 gathered on a disused runway to watch Dylan. Someone called out for everyone to sit down, and the whole crowd sat down at once as if in formation. A man in front of us had his little son on his shoulders, and kept saying to him: "That's Dylan. That's Dylan", like a mantra. The concert finished at midnight, but there was a 4-hour traffic jam to get out of the car park. I had been up all the previous night working and my memories of the concert are hazy, but at least I can say we were there.

At the end of my year at Northwick Park Hospital, Stephen asked me if I would mind if he applied there. I had obviously enjoyed it and, for his child psychiatry training, he needed to do a year of general paediatrics. I said of course I didn't mind, but the patients would all think he was me. He doubted that, but I was right on that count. Stephen enjoyed his year at Northwick Park.

Our mother Susanna was a strong woman and Steve and I both married strong women. Indeed, when Mary Cummins was his senior registrar, she once called him a bloody fool. Steve promptly said to hiself "I'm going to marry this woman". And he did. Mary and Carmel became great friends.

Most women are more industrious, more intuitive and more intelligent than most men. Our mother declined to call herself a feminist, feeling the best route was to perform well s a woman but not proselytise. However, I do not see why men cannot be feminists and I even wrote an editorial in the Journal of Paediatrics and Child Health to that effect.

When I left Northwick Park, Bernie Valman asked me if I would like to do a research project with him on children with recurrent respiratory infections. At that time, Northwick Park Hospital was allied with a Clinical Research Centre (CRC) run by the Medical Research Council. The idea was to encourage clinicians to do basic or clinical research in collaboration with colleagues working at the CRC. The model on which this was based was the successful arrangement whereby the Hammersmith Hospital was allied to a CRC. Barbara Ansell and Bernie Valman were particularly active in research that involved the CRC. Bernie would come up with promising research topics, write grants to fund the research, and then recruit a junior doctor to do the research. The junior doctor would write up the research results as scientific papers and would write an MD (Doctorate of Medicine) thesis, the medical equivalent of a PhD. One of Bernie's strongest points was that he would propose a research project that would yield interesting results whether they were positive or negative. I told Bernie that I was heading off to Australia to marry Carmel, but would return in a year to do the project with him. He agreed.

Carmel and I had plans to do some travelling on the way to Australia. We flew to New York and, despite being overcharged by a taxi-driver who dropped us on the wrong side of Central Park, we found our way to the apartment of our friends Howard and Jennifer Stringer (later Sir Howard and Lady Jennifer Stringer), who had kindly invited us to stay with them. Carmel and I visited several museums. Howard took us to Yankee Stadium to our first ever baseball game, memorable not so much for the game as for the pastrami sandwiches he bought us and for the evocative New York night skyline. Howard also helped us buy a second hand car. We headed west and found to our joy that we were driving through the Adirondack mountains in autumn, the best time to see them, when the leaves were a kaleidoscope of gold, amber, red and yellow. As we drove down a deserted highway, I said to Carmel that I would love to see a moose. Less than a mile further on, we rounded a bend and a gigantic moose was standing in the middle of the empty road. The moose stared at us for a bit before ambling unconcernedly off into the woods. We camped by a lake and went for a walk. Suddenly some beavers surfaced near us. An American camper said, "I wish I had my gun". "Yuck", said Carmel loudly. I told you I loved this woman.

We skirted the Great Lakes and crossed the prairies. The vast expanse of sky reminded me of East Africa, where you can see a similar arc of blue sky above the plains. It was a long drive across the prairies, but we weren't bored for a second. Eventually we came to the Rocky Mountains which rise majestically straight out of the prairies. We visited Banff, then drove on to Victoria, where in the anthropological museum we learned about the First Nations people, the Inuit and other Native American peoples.

Fairly exhausted by now and tired of camping, we headed straight down to Susanna in Los Angeles, where a bed awaited us. We detoured to see the Grand Canyon, which has a majesty not to be missed. After a couple of days recuperating, Carmel and I were off again. We both love ancient ruins, so decided to visit Mexico. We flew to Mexico City. We took a bus to see the pyramids at Teotihuacan. Then we travelled to Oaxaca, where women in bright reds and blues wove using back-strap looms. We went to Villahermosa, where the Olmecs carved giant heads out of stone. We went to Palenque, in the jungle, where ancient ruins are half covered by the jungle and where it was so hot and humid that we could barely drag our legs between the different ruins. We went to San Cristobal las Casas, where the men wore straw boaters with colourful ribbons dangling down their backs. But only the single men wore ribbons; as soon as they were attached their ribbons were detached.

The highlight of our trip to Mexico was the Yucatan peninsula, where we visited the ancient Mayan ruins of Chichen Itza and Uxmal. The Mayans and the Aztecs who followed them were an incongruous mixture of being brilliant mathematicians but having brutal ideas about human sacrifice. A frieze in Chichen Itza around a grass courtyard shows the courtyard was used for teams to play a popular Meso-american sport, the ball game. But at the end of the game, the captain of the winning team had the honour of having his head cut off with a stone sword by the captain of the losing side. You might think twice about winning if you were captain.

We took the bus into Guatemala. As the bus crossed the border, the clouds seemed to sink lower in the sky and form a patchy cloud cover. Carmel was intrigued by the colourful clothes worn by the Guatemalans, including young children, a mix of coloured cloth and denim.

We flew back to Los Angeles, then flew to New Zealand, a country that neither of us had ever visited. We hired a car and drove round both North and South Islands, enjoying the spectacular scenery. Then we flew across "the ditch" to Canberra, where Carmel was reunited with her parents and siblings for the first time in 3 years, and I met them for the first time. I went looking for work and found a position working in the intensive care unit of Canberra Hospital. My adult MRCP held me in good stead. It was hard work, 15 hours a day for ten days in a row, but I would earn more in those ten days than for three months' work in England, and we needed to replenish our funds after our travels.

Early one morning, on my third day in intensive care, a nurse told me that the patient I was expecting with a snakebite was arriving. I wasn't expecting the patient and thought the nurse was teasing me (as a newly arrived Pom I was fair game). An elderly woman in a wheelchair with a plastic container on her lap was wheeled down the corridor. "Oh, and I suppose that's the snake", I said pointing to the plastic container, still convinced they were joking. "Yes", said the woman and took the lid off, revealing a large snake. I was halfway down the corridor before they assured me that the snake was dead. I admitted the old woman to hospital and asked what had happened. She told me she had been admitted to a country hospital in Deniliquin with a heart attack. It was a hot day, so the doors to the outside were wide open. She fell asleep and woke to find a snake in her bed biting her finger. "So what did you do?", I asked. "I knocked it on the floor and it went under the bed. Then I rang the bell for the doctor. He came in, only a little feller like you. He looked under the bed. Then he came back with a length of hose, crawled under the bed and beat it to death. He said it was a tiger snake, gave me some anti-venom and put me in an ambulance to you." We confirmed with Canberra Zoo that it was indeed a tiger snake, an extremely venomous snake. I rang Australia's leading snake expert, who was a bit grumpy to be disturbed, but when I explained I had only been in the country for three days, he calmed down and gave me good advice. The patient didn't bat an eyelid and made a full recovery. Next day her story was front page news, which reassured me that snakebites were not likely to be an everyday occurrence in Australia.

I wanted a paediatric job. I had asked all my English colleagues for contacts before leaving, but none of them volunteered any names. But when I got to Canberra there was a letter from Mike Liberman saying he remembered working at St Mary's Hospital with an Australian doctor, Kim Oates. There was also a letter from Kim Oates saying that Mike Liberman had written to him and, as it happened, Kim ran a Child Development Unit at the Royal Alexandra Hospital for Children in Sydney. The unit catered for children with disability and their families, and Kim was looking for a Fellow for six months. This was ideal. My MRCP qualified me as a Fellow. We arranged that I come to Sydney for an interview. Kim and I warmed to each other and he offered me the position. My job was to examine and investigate children with suspected disability, counsel their parents and organise management. Kim later became Professor of Paediatrics at the University of Sydney and, when John Yu retired after moving the hospital to Westmead, Kim became Chief Executive Officer of the Royal Alexandra Hospital for Children (also called The Children's Hospital at Westmead). Kim and I also became good friends.

Carmel and I were married on February 17th, 1979. My brother and sister flew out from England. I sent Stephen into the room first. All Carmel's family (except Carmel) thought it was me. It was a bit of a mean trick, but Carmel's father George was an accomplished tease and caught me out on more than one occasion. My mother and her step-sister Ruth Obermer flew in from California, where Ruth worked as a nurse. Carmel is a Church-going Catholic and I agreed to talk to the priest before the wedding. Father Pat Power had been the chaplain at Carmel's school, became a Priest, then a Bishop and would later stand up to the Government against their mistreatment of refugees. Atheist that I am, I liked him immediately and I adore him now. He baptised our youngest child Mark and he conducted the funeral service when Carmel's father George died. Pat Power married Carmel and me in Carmel's local church, St Peter Chanel in Yarralumla.

The marriage reception was held in Carmel's parents' back yard. Circumstances meant that we were too late to find a more upmarket venue for the reception, but I preferred the informality. Our honeymoon was in the coastal town of Bateman's

Bay, in a large house belonging to a family member. Seeing how far my relatives had travelled, and since there was plenty of room, we suggested they all join us on the honeymoon. So they did, as did two of Carmel's sisters. It was perhaps one of the more crowded honeymoons ever. Ruth loved stroking the wallabies on the beach, which were surprisingly tame.

Carmel and I moved into a shared house in Bondi, a short walk from the famous Bondi Beach. There were several other lodgers, and our house was often the place for wild parties. One was a glitter party: our housemates stood on the stairs scattering handfuls of glitter onto anyone who arrived not wearing glitter. On the Sunday morning after a Saturday party, we would clean away all the empty bottles and cans while listening to Willy Nelson on the record player. I had to take three buses to reach the hospital, but it was worth it for the early morning jogs along the beach and for the early evenings lying on Bondi Beach after a hard day's work. Sometimes I would hear a 3-year-old talking on the bus and I would think "a genius". Working all day with children with severe disability can do that to you.

When it came time to counsel the parents of children with disability, I was always joined by a social worker. Julianne Mallick, whom I worked with the most, taught me by example how to raise tricky topics in a non-threatening way. "Some parents of children with disability feel guilty, even if they know it's really not their fault", she might say, and leave the statement hanging there. The parent might acknowledge that they felt that way, in which case Julianne had allowed them to legitimise their guilt. Similarly for genetic diseases, where one or both parents may feel guilty or one parent may blame the other, Julianne would raise these tricky issues with open questions which the parent might or might not explore. One day, Julianne and I were talking to a mother of a child with developmental delay. The mother described how alone she had been with her baby boy, who cried a lot. She seemed to have lacked significant family supports to help her. She described that one day the child was crying more than ever. Then he had a sudden seizure. She took him to hospital, but he had not been the same ever since. The mother cried as she related this sad story to us. Both Julianne and I thought that the mother was as good as saying that she had shaken her son and caused his brain damage. What a terrible thing for her to have to live with. It would not have helped her to ask whether she had shaken her baby, so we didn't. Sufficient, we thought, to listen sympathetically to this mother, who had not wanted to harm her baby, but had been driven to it when insufficiently supported. My time working in the Child Development Unit increased my respect for social workers immeasurably.

Carmel and David's wedding, Canberra, 1979

CHAPTER TEN: RESEARCH

After six months in Sydney, Carmel and I flew back to London for me to begin my research with Bernie Valman at Northwick Park Hospital. We bought a place to live in Cricklewood, not far from Hampstead. I was to do research on children with recurrent respiratory infections, which were most likely to be caused by viruses. Because my research involved viruses, one of my co-supervisors was Professor David Tyrrell, who first described coronaviruses. David Tyrrell had worked with my father at Mill Hill, but had now moved to Northwick Park Hospital. The research also involved children's immune response to infection, so another co-supervisor was an immunologist, Professor David Webster. Incidentally, when a friend was travelling by train in Australia, some fellow passengers asked him what he did. He told them he was an immunologist. They were amazed. They had never met someone who studied emus before. We made him a badge with a picture of an emu and "emunologist" written on it.

For my research, I recruited 30 families, each with at least two children, one of whom had recurrent respiratory infections and one of whom did not and acted as a control. When either of their children or both had a cough or cold, the families would ring me. I would drive to their home and collect respiratory specimens for viral and bacterial culture: a nose swab, a throat swab and a nasopharyngeal aspirate (snot sucked into a special container). I would make a game of collecting the specimens, pretending the child was an elephant and the nose swab was a tusk. I had a container of dry ice to keep the specimens cold while I transported them. To amuse the children, I would put a bit of dry ice on a tabletop and blow it around like a hovercraft. I enjoyed doing clinical research with children, and it helped gain their trust if I made it fun for them.

My first major paper was about children who were deficient at producing interferon. I wrote the first draft and David Tyrrell made suggestions and had me rewrite it. On the sixth version, he said it was really quite good. I asked if we could submit it. "Oh no, it's not nearly ready yet", he said. David Tyrrell finally agreed that my ninth version was ready. He sent it to the prestigious journal *The Lancet*, and they accepted it in less than a month. It was an object lesson to me about the importance of being thorough when writing scientific papers. Or books. The first reference in our *Lancet* paper was to a paper by A. Isaacs on interferon. I wished my father could have seen my *Lancet* paper. I think he would have been proud of me.

Bernie Valman was an excellent supervisor. He advised me to spend the first six months researching the field. He refused to allow me to do any clinical work at all, i.e. no on call or outpatient clinics, for a year. He said that research is hard and lonely, whereas clinical work is rewarding and seductive. In my case I am sure he was correct. I found it a slog doing the research and I would often doze off in the library. Bernie met up with me regularly, more to hear what I was doing than to tell me what to do. Bernie was very enthusiastic; I always came away from those meetings feeling more positive.

The famous statistician Doug Altman worked at Northwick Park Hospital. I went to him often for statistical help. He would never do my statistics for me, but would teach me what to do and have me do it. That was an excellent approach. Doug was a big man with a big beard. He never came in before 10am, sometimes 11am, but he was incredibly productive, authoring multiple papers and several books. Far be it from me to ask Doug what he did before 10am.

I was a proud father now, of Anna Rachel, who was born at University College Hospital, London. Carmel's mother was called Anastasia and my mother Susanna. Both of them thought Anna was named after them, and we weren't going to disabuse them. Anna was hard to settle and woke a lot in the night. Carmel and I had to get help. The paediatrician we saw suggested we split the night, which was sound advice. I would stay up with Anna until midnight or 1am. Then I would go to bed and Carmel would look after Anna until 6am. Then I took over. It was often after 9am, sometimes nearer 10am, before I reached work. Although I always got there before Doug Altman.

Paediatricians struggle when their own children are unwell: they do not want to be too involved in their child's care, but they do not want to call in the doctor (general practitioner or paediatrician) too early or too late. While I was working at Northwick Park, Bernard Valman asked me to see his daughter, whom I diagnosed correctly with appendicitis. Bernie spent the night by her bedside curled up in a chair. Later, I asked Bernie to see our infant Anna, whom he diagnosed with pneumonia and admitted to hospital for intravenous antibiotics. It took 3 months for Carmel and I to get over the exhaustion induced by Anna's illness.

Seventeen months after Anna was born, Benjamin Leonard was born at the Royal Free Hospital in Hampstead. He was called Leonard after Leonard Elmhirst. Sadly, Carmel never met Leonard. She would have loved him and he her.

An immunology professor at Northwick Park was invited to give a 30 minute talk on inflammation at Louvain, Belgium, but was unable to go. He asked me if I would give the talk instead. I said I knew nothing about inflammation, but would love to go. He told me to prepare the talk and he would help me. I wrote out a talk longhand. He told me I would send everyone to sleep if I read it out, and to come back with cue cards. I came back with several dozen cards covered in dense notes. He told me to make 30 slides, one per minute, and a maximum of 6 dot-points per slide. That way I could cue myself from the slides. I did that. He asked me if I understood one of my slides. "Not really", I admitted. "Nor do I", he said, and threw it in the bin. The speaker before me in Louvain read his talk and everyone fell asleep. I knew my slides, and was able to look at the audience as I spoke. The topic of my lecture was not very interesting, but at least nobody fell asleep.

In general I have been able to engage audiences using the technique taught me by the immunologist from Northwick Park. However, some years later I was asked to give a lecture on childhood pneumonia to the University of Sydney medical students. It was not a topic that excited me. There were about 200 students. As I droned on, they became restless and rather noisy. I walked back to my car kicking stones, angry with the students. But then I realised I had broken the cardinal rule about engaging the audience. I thought I would not be invited back next year, but in fact I was asked to lecture on childhood pneumonia again. I decided to tell the students about the Common Cold Unit in Salisbury. I had photos of the Nissen huts where volunteers were housed, including medical students I told them pointedly, and given respiratory infections. A series of experiments were carried out there, under the aegis of David Tyrrell, looking at how respiratory infections were transmitted. In one early set of experiments, two volunteers, one with a cold and the other not, played table tennis. The volunteer only caught a cold from his opponent if a fan was placed behind the player with a cold. This experiment showed that colds were airborne. A second experiment, called "the artificial sneeze", tested whether respiratory infections could be spread by droplets. A suspension of respiratory virus was drawn up into an old-fashioned bellows, then puffed into a cupboard. Immediately afterwards, a volunteer was shoved head-first into the cupboard, and told to breathe in. The volunteers exposed to the artificial sneeze caught infections, showing colds could be spread by droplets. Finally, I told them about research to test whether being cold made people more susceptible to catching colds. Researchers tried to make volunteers cold by having them stand outside on the hockey field in winter, but were unable to drop their temperatures by the desired 1°C. So they immersed the volunteers in the outdoor swimming pool with a rectal probe up their bottom until their temperature fell by 1°C. Then they tried to infect them with a respiratory virus, and discovered that they were no more susceptible to infection than controls who stayed in he warm. "You'll catch cold if you get cold" is an old wives' tale. When I finished my lecture, the students cheered. Facts are important but students like entertaining presentation of facts.

I finished my clinical research and had six months to write my doctoral thesis. I enjoyed the writing almost as much as the research. I finished writing my MD (Doctor of Medicine) thesis in the time allotted to me and submitted it.

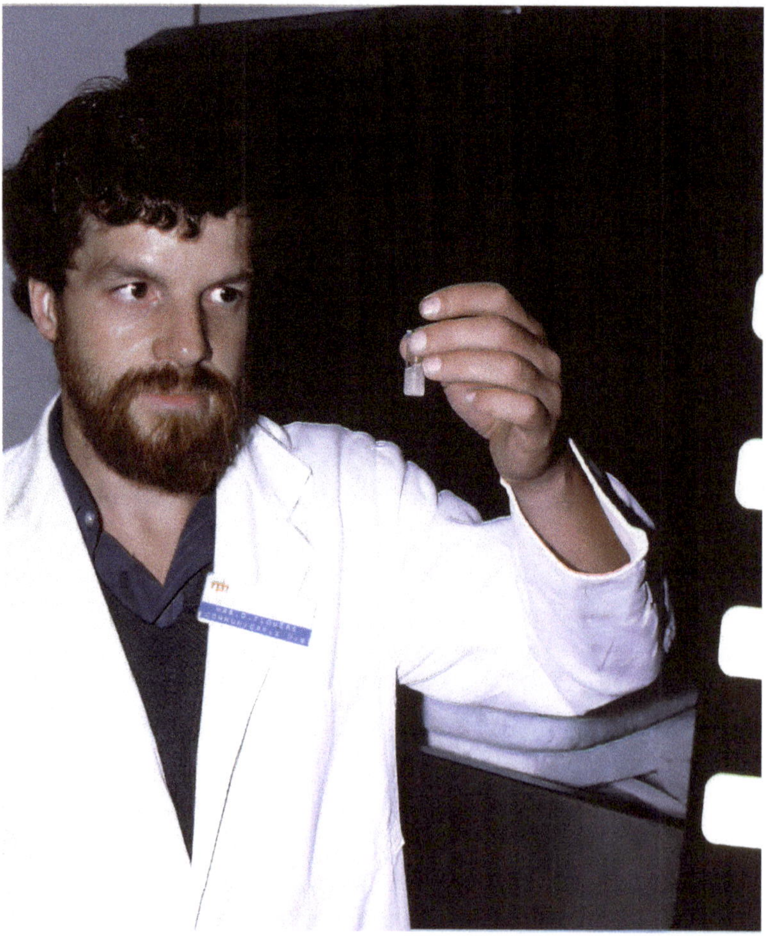

David, Northwick Park

CHAPTER ELEVEN: SYDNEY AND LONDON

Carmel needed to show her two grandchildren, Anna and Ben, to her parents in Canberra and to her siblings. I arranged to do a year at the Royal Alexandra Hospital for Children in Camperdown. I was a registrar, which is a lower position than a Fellow, which was my position when working with Kim Oates. I joked that I was sinking in rank and would be a houseman next time I worked there.

My first registrar position was in neonatology. Andrew Berry was the consultant. He was younger than me, but much more experienced, certainly in neonatology. He soon taught me how to intubate babies and I stopped being scared. It is horrible to feel that you might jeopardise a baby's health, even cost the baby's life, by failing to intubate it. Andrew went on to found NETS, the Newborn Emergency Transport Service, which transported babies from all over the state of New South Wales.

I had to fly some sick babies and children to our hospital using the Royal Flying Doctor Service. When I wrote about it to my English family, my sister replied: "I didn't know you could fly a plane." I had to explain to her that there are professional pilots who fly the planes; the doctors just look after the patients.

Carmel and I rented a house in Glebe. I walked to work although, when I had done 7 days in a row of 14 hours a day of neonatology, I could barely crawl home. I was hopeless at getting drips into tiny babies, but my saviour was a colleague, Paddy Grattan-Smith, who always succeeded. I would allow myself one failure, then ring Paddy and order him a coffee in advance payment.

One morning I received a call when I was working in the neonatal unit. Carmel had gone out the back door in her nightdress to do some washing in the outside washroom, when 2-year-old Anna had somehow locked the back door and was unable to unlock it. I rushed home with my spare set of keys to find baby Ben howling and Anna hammering on the door saying "Ope' this door, Ope' this door". Poor Carmel.

I had never done a paediatric examination and felt I needed the rigour of studying paediatrics for an examination. I decided to sit the Australian Fellowship examination while I was in Australia. It was a difficult examination, and I made things even more difficult for myself by flying to England for a job interview shortly before the examination. I wanted to work with the only paediatric infectious disease specialist in Britain, an Australian, Professor Bill Marshall at Great Ormond Street Hospital. However, competition was strong and I didn't get the job. After the interview, I had arranged to play poker with the lads. They asked me how I got on in the interview. I told them I came second. "You flew all this way to come second?" "No, I flew all this way to play poker with you." I won the first three hands, and Rosco said: "That'll get you as far as f...ing Dover".

I flew back to Australia, slept overnight and woke the day before the examination. I thought I didn't have a hope of passing. Then I told myself not to think negatively. What would help? A child with a rheumatological disorder, I thought, because I had been taught at Northwick Park Hospital by Barbara Ansell, the Queen of Rheumatology. I spent the morning before the clinical examination reading the chapter in the paediatric textbook on rheumatological disorders. When I reached the examining hospital, the child who was my "long case" was wearing splints, and I gave a little whoop. The child had a rheumatological disorder. The other thing going for me was that I had almost nothing riding on the result. If I failed it would not affect my career materially. So I passed and was FRACP (Fellow of the Royal Australasian College of Physicians).

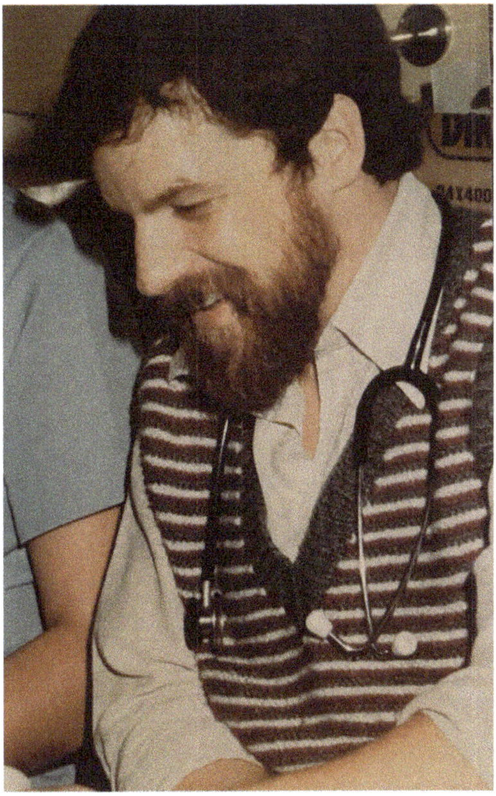

David, Camperdown

Anna went to a playgroup in Glebe, and often held onto a friend's pram on the way home in the hope of being invited back to play. One day, when we were nearing the time to fly back to London, there was a gathering in Glebe Park. Anna took me around and introduced me to the parents of all her playgroup friends. She remembered everyone's name, parents as well as children. She was three years old.

Carmel and I returned to London and I was offered a position as Lecturer in Paediatrics at Queen Elizabeth Hospital for Children, Hackney in the East End of London. I did clinical work at Queen Elizabeth Hospital, but medical students also came to the hospital, and my job was to organise their teaching. The trouble was there were two sets of students, one from The London Hospital and the other from St Bartholomew's Hospital ("Barts"). The two medical schools ran their courses one week apart and both refused to budge, so we had to give the lectures twice. Furthermore, there were two Professors, Chris Wood with an honorary position at The London Hospital medical school, aand John Walker-Smith at St Bartholomew's Hospital medical school, who would not talk to each other. I liked both of them, but they sometimes asked me to act as a go-between. I refused, thinking but not saying, that they should grow up and mend their own rift.

Carmel and I bought a house in East Finchley, a mile or so from my brother and his wife. Stephen and Mary had a daughter Catherine who was the same age as Ben. Ben and Catherine became devoted to each other. They also had a daughter Emily who was slightly older than our Tom, and used to push him around in his pushchair. Emily and Tom became very close, too.

Because I looked so like her father, Emily used to call me Davie-Daddy. In fact she still does, although she is married (ironically to a lovely man called Dave), has two children and is a consultant paediatrician.

Every month at Hackney, we had a visiting speaker. One of my responsibilities was to invite the speakers and look after them. One time, a distinguished Professor gave a talk. We had a good attendance and people asked good questions, which he answered well. A month later, police arrived at his hospital and arrested him. He used to get a lot of mail delivered to the hospital. When he was away at meetings or on holiday, he gave strict orders that nobody should open his mail. It turned out that he was being sent child pornography in the mail. He went to prison for a year, then he was sidelined into an administrative position at the Ministry of Health and forbidden from seeing children. It had never occurred to me that a paediatrician might be a paedophile.

The East End of London was the poorest part of the city. One day, a social worker I liked was in tears. I asked her what was the matter. She had been to visit a Bangladeshi family and found 13 people living in a tiny flat. When she asked how they could bear to live like this, they told her that it was better than living in Bangladesh. The pity of this had upset her terribly.

Children presented to the hospital with diseases more associated with Africa than England. I saw a lot of children with tuberculosis and several with malnutrition. I worked with Professor John Walker-Smith, a gastro-enterologist, and learned a great deal from him about gastroenteritis and cow's milk protein intolerance. His initials are J. A. W.-S. so he was often called JAWS (but not to his face). John was Australian but had become more English than the English. He had a posh English accent, he wore blue shirts with a white collar, and on his desk he had a wooden stand carrying a Union Jack and a portrait of the Queen. John used to get us, his registrars, to biopsy the small intestine of children to diagnose cow's milk protein intolerance or coeliac disease. One day, an Australian registrar Paul Jenkins told John he was scared that if he biopsied a malnourished Bangladeshi baby whom John had asked him to biopsy, he might make a hole in the bowel. To his credit, John Walker-Smith listened to Paul and changed his mind about doing the biopsy. I respected that John had the intellectual honesty to listen to junior doctors and to change his mind.

John and I became interested in an organism called Cryptosporidium, which was known to cause gastroenteritis in calves and piglets, but had recently been discovered in the stools of infants and toddlers with gastroenteritis. I decided to drive to the veterinary school in Edinburgh, to learn from a research vet how to detect the organism. I took the family. Ben showed his anxiety by saying "Ouchy, ouchy" every few minutes to ask me to stop the car so he could pass urine. He was much better on the return journey. When Susanna asked us about the journey, Anna said: "Ben needed to do wee-wee 64 times." Sue asked: "Did you get tired of it?" "We did, Ben didn't," said Anna.

Later in his career, John Walker-Smith left St Bartholomew's Hospital and moved to the Royal Free Hospital in

Hampstead. John co-authored a paper with Andrew Wakefield on gastro-intestinal changes in children with autism. The paper was published in *The Lancet*, and Wakefield used its publication to appear on television postulating a link between measles–mumps–rubella (MMR) vaccine and autism. It subsequently transpired that Wakefield had fabricated most of the data he used in the paper and that he had significant undeclared financial Conflicts of Interest. It took tireless detective work by a journalist Brian Deer to uncover the extent of Wakefield's perfidy. Falling rates of measles vaccine uptake worldwide as a direct result of the Wakefield paper resulted in many unnecessary child deaths. Wakefield was struck off the British medical register, which meant he was barred from practising as a doctor in the United Kingdom. He moved to the United States where he does not work as a doctor, but has continued to promote anti-immunisation messaging. John Walker-Smith was implicated in the fraudulent research with Wakefield. The General Medical Council (GMC) found John Walker-Smith guilty of professional misconduct and barred him from practising medicine. John appealed to the High Court, which found the GMC's arguments were simplistic and unsafe, so the Court quashed John's conviction. It was a sad and sorry end to a distinguished career.

While working at Queen Elizabeth, I negotiated to spend every Wednesday morning doing a ward round with Bill Marshall at Great Ormond Street Hospital (GOSH). I still had hopes of becoming a paediatric infectious disease specialist, but the only places I could train were in the United States or Canada, and I was not prepared to subject my Anglo-Australian family to three years in North America. I admired Bill Marshall, but sometimes I wished he had done more to establish a paediatric infectious diseases training programme in the United Kingdom. My fallback position was to be a general paediatrician with an interest in paediatric infectious diseases, like my friend Peter Rudd in Bath. Meanwhile I could enjoy learning from Bill Marshall once a week.

On one of my visits to GOSH, Bill Marshall had another visitor, a paediatric infectious disease specialist from Johns Hopkins University, Baltimore called Richard Moxon. Richard had a hybrid Anglo-American accent. After the ward round, Richard invited me for a drink at a nearby pub. Over a pint, he talked at length about his work on the molecular biology of *Haemophilus influenzae* type b (Hib), a major cause of infant meningitis, and about the development of new vaccines to prevent Hib meningitis. I did my best to keep up with what Richard was saying, but he was light-years ahead of me in thought and knowledge. I did find out that Richard was English, a Cambridge graduate, had gone to the United States to study paediatric infectious diseases, and had married the boss's daughter, Marianne.

Some months later, out of the blue, I received a phone call from the United States. It was Richard Moxon. He said I did not know him, but he had been invited to be Professor of Paediatrics at the University of Oxford. He wanted to recruit two doctors, one junior doctor to do molecular biology research with him and the other more senior doctor to do the clinical work. Richard said he had asked two friends, David Tyrrell and Bill Marshall, to recommend someone to do the clinical work and they both suggested me. I reminded Richard of our meeting in the pub and said I would be delighted to join him, subject to interview. So something *had* come up. I was going to be taught paediatric infectious diseases at Oxford by one of the world's leading paediatric infectious disease experts.

After an interview, I was offered the position of Lecturer at the John Radcliffe Hospital in Oxford. The junior position working in the laboratory was offered to Simon Kroll, who later became Professor of Paediatrics and Molecular Infectious Diseases at Imperial College, London. I played chamber music and in college concerts with Simon's wife Mary Kroll, and our children became close friends with theirs. In fact, when 5 years later we left Oxford to move to Australia, 4-year-old Tom said how much he missed Lucy Kroll.

I told Simon Kroll about my ambition to become a Professor. He said he had the same ambition, but not a Professor of Paediatrics. They had to do all the boring administration. It was much better to get a tenured position working in a hospital, and then ask the university to make you an honorary professor. That way you were a professor without the paperwork. Simon later became a professor at Imperial College, London in this way. I followed his advice and became a Professor of Paediatric Infectious Diseases without paperwork at the University of Sydney.

Shortly before I was due to start in Oxford, we found out that our house in the London borough of East Finchley (a mile from my brother's house) was riddled with dry rot. We had had two surveys performed before buying it, but both companies denied responsibility, saying the dry rot might have developed after the survey. Our friend Irma Pick had suffered from a long drawn-out and eventually unsuccessful lawsuit against Rentokil over dry rot in her Hampstead house. Big companies just keep delaying the lawsuit until you run out of money. So we knew not to seek legal redress. We hired builders to deal with the dry rot. They kept uncovering more and more dry rot. At one point we could stand on the ground floor and see the roof, three storeys above. One day, the builders took a brick out of an internal chimney and found a massive growth of fungus in the chimney cavity, like something out of *The Day of the Triffids*. The builders asked for regular payments, because a previous client had refused to pay them after they had done the work. Every week, Susanna would take between £500 and £1,000 out of the bank to pay the builders. She never once complained. In the end she lent us a total of £20,000. We often had no running water and several times I had to go round to Stephen and Mary's for a shower. For my first six months in Oxford, I commuted 60 miles driving for 90 minutes each way every day. I was driving against the traffic, so it was some solace to see the serried ranks of cars going in the other direction. I would stay overnight in Oxford if I was on call. After six months, I was completely drained. But the builders finished the work, we sold our East Finchley house, bought a cheaper one in Summertown, Oxford, and had exactly £20,000 left over. We repaid my mother the full amount she had lent us. She told us she had never expected to see the money again. How lucky were we to have had Susanna to bail us out? I dread to think what would have happened otherwise. A year later we visited the Royal Pavilion at Brighton. "Oh look", said Anna, "Dry rot". The tour guide looked a bit stunned that a 4-year-old could recognise dry rot.

David and Carmel, Cambridge

CHAPTER TWELVE: OXFORD – THE CITY OF DREAMING SPIRES

Oxford is known as the City of Dreaming Spires, which is a quote from a Matthew Arnold poem. Both Oxford and Cambridge are truly beautiful cities but Cambridge is more compact. Oxford has an ancient centre (the University of Oxford was first mentioned in the 12th century) but there is a more industrialised periphery to Oxford. Mind you, our third (Tom) and fourth (Mark) children were born at the John Radcliffe Hospital in Oxford, and with four young children, we had little time for sightseeing. Carmel much preferred Oxford to London, and we had a wonderful five years in Oxford.

Sceptics told Richard Moxon that there wouldn't be any paediatric infections in Oxford. Richard said that I should think of working with children who were particularly susceptible to infection, basically children with cancer or newborns. Oxford referred its children with cancer to London, but Sir Peter Tizard had created a world class neonatal unit in Oxford. I talked to his successor, Andrew Wilkinson, who was enthusiastic about the idea of me studying neonatal infections, as was his colleague Peter Hope, who sadly passed away far too young from cancer. I did daily ward rounds, recording data on neonatal infections, colonisation and antibiotic use. I joined the neonatal on-call roster. I renewed my friendship with William Tarnow-Mordi, who was doing research in Oxford. William is a big man and when we played squash together, I finally understood the origin of the name of the game. William liked to do his research in the quiet of the middle of the night. He was nearly nocturnal. He married Donna, later moved to the same suburb as us in Sydney and had four sons, including twin boys. Carmel and I are godparents to their youngest son, Blake. William tells me that I am allowed to be an atheist godfather because Carmel is such a good Catholic godmother.

There were hundreds of neonatologists in Britain, but not one other than me who had a special interest in neonatal infections. We in Oxford published a number of papers on neonatal infections in prestigious journals and made quite a name for ourselves, both nationally and internationally.

Richard Moxon was an invaluable teacher and mentor. When I was working with Richard on the wards, he would always ask me questions. "What is wrong with this child?" "Meningitis". "What antibiotics are you giving?" I would tell him which antibiotics. "Why?", he would ask. "Because the child has meningitis". "Yes, but why *those* antibiotics?" At first I found his "why" questions irritating, but I soon realised that Richard was exposing my lazy thinking. I automatically prescribed the antibiotics that were usually prescribed for meningitis, but had never stopped to think which organisms I was covering and whether an alternative antibiotic regimen would be preferable.

I have described already how paediatricians struggle when their own children become unwell. Richard Moxon told me one day that his preschool age son had croup, a common but occasionally serious childhood viral infection for which antibiotics have no role. I asked him what he did. He said it got worse at night, so they called the doctor. Marianne answered the door and Richard hid under the bedclothes while the GP prescribed antibiotics. Did he give the antibiotics? Yes, even though he knew they were unnecessary. It is different when it is your own child.

We wanted to start a weekly teaching round on paediatric infectious diseases. We wanted to present clinical cases but we had relatively few children, other than neonates, with infections. We, therefore, approached our adult infectious disease colleague Tim Peto, now Professor of Medicine at the University of Oxford, and asked if the adult team would like to present alternate weeks with the paediatric team. We learned a lot from each other. That model worked so well that I used it when I moved permanently to Sydney.

Simon Kroll was working successfully with Hib in Richard's molecular biology laboratory. There was now an effective Hib vaccine which would prevent around 1200 Hib cases in young children in the United Kingdom every year—900 of them meningitis—and around 600 Hib cases a year in Australia. Yet the Hib vaccine was being used in the United States, but not yet in Britain or Australia. It seems that people have to see local data for themselves and will not be persuaded by overseas data. Richard lobbied hard and educated hard. He started studies of Hib vaccine in England to show that the vaccine would protect infants. Robert Booy, later Professor in Sydney, and Andy Pollard, later Sir Andy Pollard after his ground-breaking work developing a COVID-19 vaccine, collaborated with Richard on Hib vaccine studies. Hib vaccines are now routinely incorporated in the routine infant immunisation schedule in Britain and Australia.

We had a patient with an infection that was difficult to treat. Eventually she went home. Later that week I had a call from the man on the front desk, saying there was something there for me, but he wouldn't allow it into *his* hospital. Puzzled, I went to the front desk and found the girl's family had left two pheasants for us. Richard wanted no part of it, so I took the two pheasants home. My research told me I had to hang them until the pheasants were dripping. I hung them outdoors because Carmel wouldn't let them in the house. When they were dripping, we invited Richard and Marianne round for a meal. The pheasants were really quite tasty.

Richard thought I should work with the laboratory scientists in the Institute of Molecular Medicine, which was on the same campus as the John Radcliffe Hospital. Seeing my reluctance, he suggested I should at least go and listen to a lecture there. I went to hear Professor Andrew McMichael give a lecture on the immune response to influenza. Andrew was a world leader on the T-lymphocyte (T-cell) response to influenza. I understood half of the lecture if I'm lucky, but I was intrigued. In Andrew's laboratory, I met a young scientist called Charles Bangham. Charles's father was an endocrinologist at Mill Hill and knew my father. I didn't know Charles, but his sister and mine had been schoolfriends. I was told a story that Charles, who loved to travel, found an endocrinologist called Tony Hope who wanted to study whether people in the Andes were less fertile than lowlanders. In the story, Charles and Tony travelled to the Andes, then wrote a paper called *The effect of altitude on fertility* by Bangham and Hope. Charles insists the story is apocryphal, but I recounted it during a live radio interview, so it must be true. Anyway, Charles is a very unconventional and original thinker. When he worked in Mill Hill, everyone was working on influenza viruses. To be different, Charles started working on respiratory syncytial virus (RSV). RSV is an interesting virus which infects almost all infants, often causing a disease called bronchiolitis, but can still infect adults into old age. Bronchiolitis is one of the most common reasons for children being admitted to hospital during the winter months. I discovered that Charles knew a lot about growing RSV and a lot about T-cells, but he had never seen an infant with bronchiolitis. In fact, I found that, while I was a bit reticent about the science, the scientists were a bit in awe of clinicians. I took Charles to see some infants with bronchiolitis. He taught me how to grow RSV and how to isolate T-cells from someone's blood. We collaborated on a research project: I took blood, with parental permission of course, from infants with bronchiolitis. Together Charles and I studied whether the infants' T-cells could recognise other cells infected with RSV. They often could. This was an important finding, showing that even very young infants had an active T-cell immune response. We published our findings in the prestigious medical journal *The Lancet*.

In the Institute of Molecular Medicine, I met Alain Townsend, who was doing extremely important work on the way T-cells recognise influenza-infected cells and kill them (so-called killer T-cells). Alain's work had major implications for the way T-cells recognise foreign cells in general. Alain's wife Erin is an excellent artist. Indeed, she gave us a beautiful painting of the Oxfordshire landscape which hangs in a prominent position in our house. Erin's father was Sir Roger Bannister, the first sub-four minute miler. When we were in Oxford, Sir Roger was the Master of Pembroke College, Oxford. One morning Alain came to work looking downcast. When I asked him why, he said: "My children drew on their grandparents' walls." "Children will be children," I said. "Of Queen's College", he said. "With indelible markers". Queen's College, Oxford was founded in 1341, although the wood panelling on which they drew is thought to date from the 18th century.

I also met Frances Gotch, who began working in Andrew McMichael's laboratory as a bottle washer, became a lab technician, completed a PhD with Andrew and became a Professor of Immunology at Imperial College, London. What a meteoric rise. She and her husband Mike, an architect, became firm friends of ours.

The Institute of Molecular Medicine had a huge tea-room. Everybody would time their experiments so they could have morning tea together. The conversation was lively and exciting. I recommended building a similar area when they were building the new children's hospital at Westmead in Sydney, but got a room less than half the size. The scientists were passionate about their subject. When philosopher and academic Sir Karl Popper was giving a talk in London, several of them drove 60 miles each way to hear him talk.

There was time for leisure, too. Andrew McMichael and his wife Kate lived in a village near Oxford. One evening several of us from the laboratory drove to his house and Andrew took us out for a walk to hear the nightingales sing.

Charles and I used to drive to the Common Cold Research Unit on Salisbury plain, not far from Stonehenge, to infect adult volunteers with RSV and test their immune response. A Canadian paediatrician Noni MacDonald came to visit the paediatric infectious disease department in Oxford and joined Charles and me on some of our trips to Salisbury. Noni is very short and I have fond memories of her wearing a white hospital robe that reached the ground, wandering the alleyways of the Common Cold Research Unit, like a white Dalek.

Many distinguished visitors came to Oxford, including future Australian of the Year Fiona Stanley and her microbiologist husband Geoff Shellam. One day, Richard Moxon and his wife Marianne invited Carmel and me to their house to meet one of his erstwhile colleagues, Hamilton Smith. Carmel talked to his wife, or rather listened to her as she boasted in her Texan accent: "When Ham did this..." and "When Ham did that..." and "When Ham got the Nobel Prize". "Ooh. Did your husband get the Nobel Prize?" said Carmel. "Can I touch him?" As luck would have it, there was a lull in the conversation that coincided with Carmel's words, which echoed round the room. Ham, his wife and I thought it was hilarious, but Richard and Marianne looked a bit pained.

Our two younger sons, Tom and Mark, were born in the John Radcliffe Hospital in Oxford. Our children loved Carmel's younger brother Billy who worked as a fireman in Canberra. and used to get them to call him "top bloke". Billy played cricket with them when they were in Canberra. While we were in Oxford, Billy was killed in a car crash, the day before his 25th birthday. No matter how hard we tried, we were unable to get Carmel a flight to Australia to attend Billy's funeral. Carmel was pregnant with Mark when Billy died.

I structured my days to arrive early so I could be home in time to read to the children. I read to them in bed with one child either side, snuggling up to me. Because of the spread of their ages, I read to Anna and Ben first; later I read Tom and Mark the most successful of the books. An early favourite was Lewis Carroll's *Alice's Adventures in Wonderland*. Mark loved the John Tenniel illustrations, and would always ask me to turn to the one of Alice with her neck elongated after drinking a potion. This would send Mark into helpless giggles, which set us all off laughing. Sometimes I was exhausted from work and would nod off while reading. Once when that happened, Anna whispered in my ear: "This is the voice of your conscience speaking." Apparently it is a line from *Dumbo*, a film the children used to watch at their grandmother's. I read *The Lord of the Rings* by JRR Tolkien when I was in Paris, age 18, and loved it. I tried Anna and Ben on Tolkien's *The Hobbit*, which was a success, although I edited out long, descriptive passages which were better for atmosphere than adventure. So we progressed to read the whole of *The Lord of the Rings*, using the same editing. I then read Mark Twain's *Tom Sawyer* and *Huckleberry Finn*. By then Anna and Ben were reading to themselves, so I started reading to Tom and Mark. One evening, Carmel came into the bedroom saying she was sceptical that 5-year-old Mark was old enough for *The Lord of the Rings*. I asked the boys: "Who do you think that was just coming out of the woods dressed in white?" "That would be Saruman, Dad", said Mark and Tom nodded. "OK," said Carmel.

My position was not permanent and Richard Moxon made it clear, and quite rightly so, that I needed to apply for funding. My least favourite part of research is applying for grants. However, on this occasion, I somehow managed to cobble together an application and was awarded a prestigious Wellcome Senior Lecturer position for two years. I think the Wellcome must have been influenced by the strength of my collaborators.

One day Richard asked me how I was going. "Not so well", I said. "I am worried about the progress of my research and I can't sleep for worrying where my next grant is coming from". "Oh good", he said. "Then you're really getting into it." From that day, I vowed to myself that I would get a tenured clinical position so that I would never again be consumed by worry about getting grants.

My senior lecturer position came with honorary consultant status. To my surprise, I found that the responsibility of making clinical decisions as a consultant weighed much more heavily than as a senior registrar. It should have been obvious to me that the buck stops with the consultant. I coped passably well until a 14-year-old girl was admitted to intensive care under my care with unexplained coma. She needed intubation and artificial ventilation, but this resulted in severe pneumonia. I asked everyone I could think of for advice. Richard always asked his colleagues, even rang them in the United States, whenever he wanted advice. What worried me was that this girl was dying and that maybe a better clinician than I was might have been able to save her. I slept very poorly and sometimes went into the intensive care in the middle of the night. As a last desperate measure, I arranged for her to be transferred to London for a heart and lung transplant, but she died in the ambulance on the way to London. I went to her funeral. I was struggling and had a near breakdown. Richard Moxon and I walked along a towpath by the River Isis, while I told him of my problems. He told me I must take a week off and must go and see someone. I took a week off and booked to see a wonderful Oxford psychotherapist, Isabel Menzies, a friend of my mother. By the time I saw Isabel, I had slept well and was already feeling better. She reassured me that my response to the recent stresses of a dying patient and Billy's death was only to be expected. She knew my family history, but did not see this "wobble" as a danger sign. I was very relieved, and returned to work, grateful to Richard for being so solicitous and giving such wise advice.

In continuing my research work into RSV, I decided that, because it is a winter virus, I could go to Sydney in the Australian winter and so get three winters and three RSV epidemics in a row. That way I could also introduce our Oxford-born children, Tom and Mark, to their Australian grandparents and aunts and uncle. I arranged to work with immunologist Andrew Kemp at the Royal Alexandra Hospital for Children in Camperdown. Carmel and I found a house to rent near the hospital and we enrolled Anna and Ben in Forest Lodge Primary School, which was next to the hospital. The children and I walked to their school every morning. We passed a sweet smelling lemon tree, and we would sing "Lemon tree". We also passed the Arnott's biscuit factory with its wonderful aromas.

Although my research was not particularly productive, the trip to Sydney was very productive. The Chief Executive Officer of the hospital, John Yu, approached me. If I ever wanted to set up a paediatric infectious disease department, he told me, he would welcome me and would give me up to $500,000 for research. This was the clinical position with tenure that I had craved.

We returned to Oxford to finish my lectureship. We discussed the possible move to Sydney in great depth. Oxford was not offering me a position and there was no infectious disease position available elsewhere in the United Kingdom. What is more, Carmel had been in England for ten years. Surely I owed it to her to be close to her parents and her siblings. Carmel said that if we moved it had to be a permanent move.

We decided to move to Australia for the long term. I contacted John Yu who was as good as his word. The position was advertised, I was interviewed over the telephone and offered the position.

Carmel and David with Tom, Anna, Ben, and Mark

Dave, Carmel, Anna, Ben and the UK crowd, 1989

CHAPTER THIRTEEN: A NEW BEGINNING IN SYDNEY

We sold our Oxford house and moved to Sydney in 1989. Initially, we lived in rented accommodation in Glebe. At the hospital, I met a young doctor, David McIntosh, and found he owned a magnificent mid-19th century mansion, Margaretta Cottage, in the same street as our rental house. David owned a harpsichord, a 19th century Dutch organ and two pianos. He was generous enough to allow our children to play on the instruments, and they were respectful of their precious nature. David has organised the Glebe Music Festival for over 30 years, a phenomenal achievement. Our favourite concerts are the ones he holds in Margaretta Cottage, the perfect venue for chamber music. After six months, we moved to a Federation House in Eastwood. Eastwood is noted for Granny Smith, a fruit-grower, who gives her name to the crisp green Granny Smith apple. Eastwood holds an annual Granny Smith festival.

I had intended to set up a Department of Immunology and Infectious Diseases with Andrew Kemp as the immunologist and me as the infectious disease physician. It made sense to link the two disciplines which are intimately related: children with infections mount a protective immune response and children with impaired immunity get infections with so-called opportunistic organisms that do not usually cause infections in healthy children. However, Andrew Kemp had accepted a position as Professor of Immunology at the Royal Children's Hospital, Melbourne. His planned replacement, Dr Alyson Kakakios, was on maternity leave. I had started a Department of Immunology and Infectious Diseases, but I was the only member. The name of my Department was longer than all its members. I had done some immunology during my research at Northwick Park Hospital, so was able to supervise the immunology laboratory until Alyson returned from maternity leave. I was responsible for infection control, and worked closely with the hospital infection control sister, Di Dalton. I saw children referred because of unusual or severe infections. I attended the chest X-ray meetings and clinical meetings, mainly with colleagues I knew from previous visits. I learned a lot and made a lot of good friends.

The hospital was due to move from Camperdown to Westmead after 7 years. Recognising that we were in it for the long haul, we looked for a house equidistant between the two sites. Carmel found a house for sale in Eastwood and asked my opinion. When I saw the garden I told her this has to be the right place for us. Carmel asked why I was so sure without even seeing the inside. I said it had a huge Sydney blue gum and a large oak tree, so it had the perfect symbolism for our marriage. The house itself was a lovely Federation house, built in 1913, older than our house in Oxford.

It took me a while to get used to living in Sydney. Instead of the lyrical dawn chorus of Oxford, we were woken every Sydney morning by a dawn cacophony of cackling kookaburras, of koels (a species of long-tailed cuckoo) which from dawn every spring call with a persistent ko-el that grates on the nerves, and the appropriately named noisy miners. In high summer, you can add the continual scratching sound made by the grating legs of the cicadas.

My mother was furious with me for moving overseas and took it personally. According to her, we had moved to avoid her. Every week, she wrote me abusive letters which would upset me. Carmel told me not to read them, but I kept hoping my mother would mellow. For over 20 years, I wrote a hand-writtten letter every week to my mother and one to my sister Harriet, until they died. For 35 years, I have also written at least one letter a week to my brother Stephen, who writes even more prolifically in reply.

My contract allowed me to travel overseas business class every two years to attend a meeting. I told the hospital I would like to go economy class and take one of my children, which would be cheaper for them than a business class fare. The hospital administration showed admirable flexibility in letting me do this. When Anna was 9 years old I went to the British Paediatric Association (BPA) meeting in York and left Anna with my mother. Two years later I brought Ben, then Tom, then Mark. They all loved staying with their grandmother and she loved them and spoilt them something rotten. Each time I went to the BPA meeting in York. My mother saw these visits as a peace offering and her letters softened. I wrote to my mother once a week until she died. I also wrote a letter to Stephen and a letter to Harriet once a week for over 30 years. In all I wrote over 5,000 handwritten letters to them. I still write to Stephen and Mary at least once a week.

Carmel and I had agreed that if we moved to Australia it would be a permanent move. Nevertheless, from time to time I would get the "existential agonies" and pine for Oxford. I would ask Carmel: "What if Richard Moxon moves and the Professor of Paediatrics job in Oxford becomes available?" She would say: "We won't argue about it. *You* can go". "What about the children?" I would ask. "We won't fight over them," she would say. "You can have them all". That would shut me up for a few months.

About two years after we moved to Sydney, my brother had a psychotic episode. He was almost 42 years old, the same age at which my father Alick had his first episode. Stephen was admitted to mental hospital where he was sedated, too heavily, so that he could hardly speak. Our friend David Redman, the anaesthetist, visited him, then spoke to his doctors. Luckily they listened to David and lightened the sedation, freeing Stephen. I felt terribly guilty that our move to Australia might have contributed to Stephen's breakdown. He was diagnosed with bipolar disorder, like our father Alick; there is a strong genetic component to bipolar disorder. Now it was my turn to have a sword of Damocles hanging over me. It was surely only a matter of time before I had a psychotic episode. Stephen was started on lithium preventive therapy. He has had two more psychotic episodes since, and has been generally well. Susanna, however, was so worried that her patients would find out about Stephen's illness that she said to him: "I wish you had never been born". In his autobiography *On the Move – A Life*, neurologist and author Oliver Sacks writes that his mother said the same thing to him when he told her he was homosexual. He writes that he forgave her, but he certainly never forgot. Words are very powerful. When used as weapons, it is hard to take them back.

Early one morning, I walked into a long, narrow corridor which led to the Emergency Department. Suddenly I heard shouting down the end of the corridor followed by two loud bangs. It was only when the smell of cordite reached me that I was sure they were gunshots. A uniformed guard fell to the ground. Two men dressed all in black and wearing black balaclava helmets came running towards me. At least one of them was carrying a sawn-off shotgun. There were sounds like bees around my head. A woman with a baby in a pushchair moaned and threw herself protectively over her baby. I stepped aside into an alcove to let the men run past. A second guard stepped outdoors and fired shots after the fleeing men. It turned out that the two men in black had been trying to rob the Securicor guards as they collected money from a building society office in the corridor. The Securicor guard who was hit luckily escaped with only minor injury. The other Securicor guard had been firing recklessly down the corridor at the robbers, endangering the lives of patients and staff. The sounds like bees were bullets, which we found embedded in the walls and ceiling. For once I was glad to be Little Davie; had I been taller I would likely have collected a bullet.

I felt secretly ashamed. The woman with the baby had shown great courage and wonderful maternal instinct. I had been paralysed by fear. That day, I had to give a statement to the police at police headquarters, although I returned to counsel a family with a genetically determined defect of immunity because they had driven a long way from the country for the appointment.

Carmel and Dave

Ralph Hanson, the Head of the Emergency Department, called a meeting the next day to debrief. Nowadays, the value of debriefing is questioned because, for some people, it causes them to ruminate rather than recover. I found the debrief very helpful, in the short term at least. Ralph pointed out that our families would not thank us if we got ourselves killed being brave. Many of the staff were very shocked by the shooting. One nurse tried to dive under a bench and dislocated her shoulder. There was strength to be had in sharing our experiences.

I had great trouble getting off to sleep for months afterwards. Whenever I closed my eyes I could see men in black running towards me. I suffered from nightmares. Whenever I saw a Securicor van or a policeman with a gun, it made me very uncomfortable. This lasted two years. Just as I was getting better, I was subpoenaed to appear in court for the trial of the two would-be robbers. I started getting nightmares again. But when I got to court, the two men were behind a bullet-proof glass panel. One of them looked like how I imagined "Injun Joe" from *The Adventures of Tom Sawyer* by Mark Twain would look. That was a book I had read to my children. Somehow that took away the mystique and took away my nightmares. I didn't tell my children what had happened because I was afraid of scaring them. The episode had such a profound effect on me that I couldn't help thinking of the profound and lasting effect war trauma has on military personnel. Carmel's father, George, was a 19-year-old tail gunner in World War II. He never talked to his family about the war, but he suffered from anxiety all his life, which must surely have been exacerbated by his traumatic war experience. I am thankful that none of my immediate family has been directly exposed to war, and I hope with all my heart that they never will be.

We used to drive to Canberra every few months to visit Carmel's parents, George and Stasia. After supper, I liked to take the children for a walk. One warm autumn evening, I was walking in a little nearby wood with all four children, when Mark aged about 3, said he was scared of the wolf. I tried to reassure him that there aren't any wolves in Australia, but to no avail, so I carried him. His three older siblings went on ahead and hid in the bushes making howling noises, the little angels. Mark clung tightly to me. As we neared the end of the walk, Tom aged 5, walked closer to me. At the end, I said to Mark: "There, we didn't meet any wolves." "No", said Tom, "but I met my imagination."

I would watch Tom and Mark play soccer every Saturday. When Tom was 12, his coach resigned and I took over as coach of his team. They played on Saturdays and I trained with them for two hours on Tuesdays. We worked our way up from the 4th division to the top division. We won the 2nd division final; Tom played at full back and made a goal-saving tackle just before halftime when we were leading 1–0. All the team congratulated him. Next year, we lost every game in the top division, which was a test of our resilience. But we were promoted again the next year and, in our final season when the boys were about to leave school, came mid-table in the top division. Somewhat to my surprise, I enjoyed interacting with adolescent boys. One time I was watching a game so intently, that I walked into a pole. A bit later I called out to one of our players to concentrate. He shouted back that it was more fun watching me walking into poles. Touché. For Tom and me, our shared soccer team was cement for our relationship.

Mark was a very good soccer player, both indoor (Futsal) and outdoor. He played Futsal for New South Wales, Mark's NSW Futsal team won the national interstate championships and Mark, aged 15, went on a tour playing Futsal in Brazil and Argentina with the NSW Futsal team.

Mark also played club cricket every Saturday morning for Epping as a spinner and opening batsman. His club coach Steve Brompton was a high school teacher and MG fanatic. I was the scorer and wrote the weekly match report. Denis Crowcroft was the umpire. Steve's son Hugh and Denis's son Steve also played in the team. One evening a week, Steve, Denis and I would meet to plan the batting order and the bowling order. Steve was scrupulously fair, and made sure every boy got the same number of innings and the same number of overs to bowl. This allowed some boys who were initially weak players the opportunity to thrive. For example, Will, the son of my friend Peter van Asperen, a paediatric respiratory physician at the Children's Hospital at Westmead, an erratic bowler who bowled many wides, settled down and became an accomplished spin bowler. Tragically, both Steve Brompton and Peter van Asperen died far too young from pancreatic cancer.

Twice we played against a team which included a 9-year-old Somali player who had lost a leg to a landmine. He had a prosthetic leg, but preferred to play without it, hopping to bat, bowl and field. Like our team, he was given every chance. When he scored his first ever run, parents and players on both sides cheered.

A colleague told me he hated cricket at school because he always fielded on the boundary and was never given a chance to bat or bowl. He was very impressed when I described Steve Brompton's approach.

One day, our family was driving home from a family visit

and we stopped for a break. Mark and I climbed a hill. "Race you down, Dad", called Mark. I went perilously straight down the hill. Mark took the longer, safer road but caught his leg in a cattle grid and sustained a greenstick fracture, which kept him in plaster and on crutches for six week. Mark's comment was: "At least it wasn't the soccer season, Dad."

Our eldest child, Anna, was a beautiful, bright child, but a rebellious teenager. She hated her girls only secondary school, and precipitated her leaving the school by lighting the underside of her desk with a cigarette lighter during a lesson. She switched to a co-educational school which suited her better. She would often stay out late "clubbing" with friends, which gave her parents sleepless nights waiting to hear her return. Aged 15, Anna told me University was my f...ing agenda and said she wanted to leave home. Carmel came up with a brilliant solution: she paid for our garage to be converted into a large room with shower and toilet. Anna moved into the "cottage" and told her friends she had moved out. Carmel and I no longer felt the need to listen out at night for Anna's return. Anna completed school and qualified for an arts degree. After a year she switched to psychology and won the Dean's award for star student in psychology. The university psychologists wanted Anna to do a PhD, but Anna had decided to study for medical school admission. She worked in the Department of Public Health of the University of Sydney as a research assistant on a project screening for bowel cancer, while studying for the admission examination to study medicine. She was accepted to study medicine at the University of Sydney, and specialised as a surgeon. She told me with a grin that when I told her she was going to be a surgeon, I said: "Oh dear. So you're not going to be part of the caring profession". Anna is a deeply caring as well as a highly competent surgeon. She specialised as an upper gastrointestinal surgeon, a highly competitive specialty, and is a consultant on the Gold Coast. She also teaches medical students attending Bond University.

As we had done in Oxford, I set up meetings with my adult colleagues, Don Packham, Richard Benn, Tom Gottlieb, Lyn Gilbert, and Tania Sorrell, where adult and paediatric infectious disease specialists would present alternate weeks. One day, a paediatric surgeon John Harvey whom I knew from Oxford, asked me if I would see a little boy who had been bitten by a shark. John said the boy's wound was smelling "a bit fishy." The wound grew unusual organisms. I thought this was a unique case to present to our adult colleagues. But before I could present our little boy, the adult team presented a young man who, one night, under the influence of alcohol, had gone swimming in the Parramatta River. Not only did he have teeth marks up his thigh where a bull shark bit him, but his testis was hanging out of his scrotum. Fortunately, this was a problem easily rectified. We wrote the cases up. David Burgner suggested the title "Just when you thought it was safe to get back into the water" (a line from the movie *Jaws*). The journal had no sense of humour and, to my chagrin, published it as "Shark bites in Australia".

I was friends with Kaye Flugelman, who worked in the Art Department of the Children's Hospital. One day she told me that a sculpture done by her father, the famous sculptor Bert Flugelman, had been removed from its majestic position at the top of Martin Place, by the Lord Mayor of Sydney Frank Sartor, and was lying in a building site, where it had been damaged by a reversing truck. The sculpture was called *Pyramid Tower*, and consisted of a 19 metre high tower of stainless steel pyramids and tetrahedra. Bert had won a commission to build the sculpture, which was to honour the great Australian artist William Dobell. Sartor did not like the sculpture, which he called the "silver shish kebab". I wrote a letter questioning Sartor's right to be the arbiter of artistic taste. The letter was published in the Sydney Morning Herald and, whether or not my letter had anything to do with it, Bert's sculpture was repaired and moved to the corner of Pitt and Spring Street, where it catches the green and yellow city lights to great advantage.

Bert invited Carmel and me to visit him in his house in Jamberoo. We became friends and visited him a number of times. I even took my mother to visit the charismatic sculptor. Lyrebirds ran across the road as we approached his house in the rain forest. Bert was a wonderful raconteur. He told us that he entered a competition for a sculpture to grace Rundell Mall, a pedestrian shopping precinct in Adelaide. Bert built two massive silver globes one on top of the other. He called the sculpture: *On further reflection*. However, the day the sculpture was exhibited for the first time, the Adelaide Advertiser front page showed a photo of the sculpture with the headline "Bert's Balls in the Mall", a name it has retained ever since. Bert would tell that story with a wicked grin.

Bert was always wicked. One time the PBAC held a special meeting in Bowral, where Bert and Rosie were now living. I went to visit Bert, whom Kaye told me was feeling old and a bit down. I took along a beautiful, young PBAC member, Karen Peachey. Bert flirted with Karen outrageously in front of Rosie. At one point he patted the sofa next to him and asked Karen to come and sit next to him. "You *must* be joking," she said. Bert just grinned.

I told a Camperdown colleague who held a senior position in the Royal Australasian College of Physicians, Peter Procopis, that I thought the Australasian clinical examination was too hard. Candidates were examined as if they were about to become consultants, when in fact they were about to enter three years of advanced paediatric training. Peter made sure I was appointed to the RACP Examinations Committee to argue my point. With the aid of influential colleagues such as Mike South and Andrew McDonald who held the same view, we succeeded in changing the level expected of candidates to a more realistic one. Later, I became Chair of the Written Examinations Committee, which wrote multiple choice questions for the first written part of the RACP examination. Our meetings to discuss questions were long but highly informative; I tried my hardest to make them fun. One year the meeting was held in Melbourne. As we passed the College of Surgeons, Julie Bines, a female paediatric gastro-enterologist, said she would like to go to the toilet. Remembering my mother's experience at her London examination, I warned Julie, tongue in cheek, that they might not have a ladies' toilet. "Don't be so stupid, David", she said. "This is Melbourne." She emerged with a wry grin on her face. "Well?" I asked. "They do have a ladies' toilet, but it has urinals with flowerpots in them." We all got the giggles.

The Chair of the Written Committee is automatically appointed to the Clinical Examinations Committee, and has to travel the country with colleagues from the committee examining candidates in different hospitals. The candidates see two "long cases" for an hour each, taking a history from the parent (usually the mother) or carer and examining the patient. They also see four "short cases" where they are given 15 minutes to examine one system on a child, e.g. a cardiac or a neurological examination. The examiners see the long and short cases before the candidate. A colleague and friend Mike South and I always insisted that the examiners should take the history and see the patients for the short cases blind without any prior patient notes, to be fair to the candidates. If the examiners could not get the diagnosis unaided, it was unfair to expect the candidates to get it right. There was enormous camaraderie between the examiners as we travelled to Perth, Darwin, Townsville, Geelong, Brisbane, Melbourne, Sydney, Newcastle and New Zealand examining with local examiners on local patients. I learned a huge amount of theory from being on the written examination committee and a huge amount of clinical medicine from being on the clinical committee. Furthermore, I learned that the parents and carers of children with severe disability are the unsung heroes of our society. I taught our own candidates that a medical student could take a simple history of the events in the child's life. However, an RACP candidate needed to ask questions in depth to find out the effects of the child's illness on the child and on the whole family. For example, when the child had a condition such as cerebral palsy, I stressed that we should ask the parents if they have back pain, which could be due to lifting the child and improved with simple, practical measures such as providing hoists and making sure the parents use them. The examination aims to teach candidates a holistic view of what it means for a family to have a child with major disabilities. Hopefully it also teaches candidates and examiners humility.

One year I was scheduled to examine in Perth and arranged to stay with dear friends David Burgner, a paediatric infectious disease specialist and researcher (now Professor), Martha Hickey, a specialist obstetrician/gynaecologist and researcher (also now a professor) and their young children Claudia, Conrad and Milo (all now charming young adults). The family's *au pair* was desperately homesick and never smiled. I woke early on the morning of the clinical examination and the children were also awake. In the dressing up box I found a bra, made from two half-coconut shells, and a grass skirt. The poor *au pair* came into the room just as I was shimmying from side to side, teaching the children how to dance the hula. She looked shocked and left. I spent the day examining at the children's hospital. At the end of the day, I found a text message from David Burgner saying: 'The *au pair* has resigned. I blame the hula'. The next time I went to see the family, the children all called me "Dave Isaacs, the *au pair* scarer", and that remains my nickname with the family to this day.

The hospital move from Camperdown to Westmead was a monumental effort. The new hospital had a new name, The Children's Hospital at Westmead (although it is still also the Royal Alexandra Hospital for Children). The new hospital has spectacular modern art. The canny CEO, John Yu, himself a collector of modern art, had the brilliant idea of forming an Arts Committee and inviting Joanna Capon, wife of Sir Edmund Capon, then Director of the Art Gallery of New South Wales, to chair the committee. Joanna put gentle pressure on contemporary artists to donate their paintings and sculptures to the hospital. The hospital was designated an art gallery, which meant the artists got tax relief for their donations. Michael Johnson generously donated a massive painting, which I love, called *Homage to Miles Davis*. It looks a little like a Jackson Pollock painting, but a bit more ordered, with lines dancing across the canvas like music. Michael told Joanna that she had hung the painting too low, so that children would touch it and damage it. "Then take it back," she told him. "If it's too high the children won't be able to see it. I want the children to interact with the artworks". Michael Johnson gave in. The picture is the highlight of the gallery at the main entrance of the hospital. In 20 years, I have never once seen a child touch it.

Joanna Capon looked after the artworks, commissioned new artworks and moved them around. She had a label backed with Velcro on the wall next to each artwork, giving the title and the artist, but mischievous children would swap the titles around, so she left the works unattributed. Joanna started an annual competition for primary school children in New South Wales, called Art Express. Several hundred submissions arrive every year. The 50 best paintings are selected to tour the state and are displayed in the local children's hospitals. The walls of The Children's Hospital at Westmead showcase some of these artworks. I was lucky enough to be asked to be a judge on a few occasions. The judges have to select their 50 favourites from some 700 admissions. Last year I was a judge. I stepped aside to let a slightly older man into the hall. "Hello", I said. "I'm David Isaacs. Do I know you?" "I'm Ken Done", he said. "Of course you are", I said sheepishly. He was a fellow judge. No wonder I thought I had seen him before. Tony Delamothe and I both have reproductions of a Ken Done painting on our wall.

When I became Editor-in-Chief of the Journal of Paediatrics and Child Health (JPCH), I wanted to make the journal more colourful. I arranged with Joanna and her team that they would send me photographs of the 50 best artworks from Art Express to be published in the journal. The children and their parents submitting artworks all gave permission for the artworks to be reproduced, so I had no problem with copyright.

I wrote an editorial about Malpa, a charity organisation that teaches Indigenous and non-Indigenous children how to be young doctors, an Indigenous concept. This programme improves Indigenous school attendance significantly. The founders of Malpa asked me to join the Board of Malpa, something I thoroughly enjoyed.

Many of the staff, including me, felt mentally and physically drained by the move to Westmead, in the same way that moving house is a stressful life event. Westmead was much bigger than Camperdown, with a much bigger catchment area, which has pluses and minuses. The hospital acquired new colleagues who had been working in the paediatric department of the adult Westmead Hospital. Peter McIntyre, an expert on the epidemiology of Hib, joined Alyson Kakakios and me in the expanding Department of Immunology and Infectious Diseases. But the move lost us some of the close camaraderie of Camperdown, where everyone knew everyone, and where the respiratory team of Craig Mellis, Peter van Asperen and Henry Kilham (the last two now sadly deceased) met for morning coffee after their ward round and welcomed outsiders like me.

Preeti Joshi was my first ever PhD candidate and Alyson was her co-supervisor. Preeti succeeded in writing her PhD thesis and joined the Department as an allergist. Allergy rapidly became the commonest reason for an outpatient visit. Allergy was not my forte, and we decided to form two new Departments. Alyson Kakakios, Melanie Wong, Diane Campbell and Preeti Joshi formed the Department of Allergy and Immunology. Virologist and clinician Alison Kesson headed a new Department of Microbiology and Clinical Infectious Diseases. Alison and I were joined by Ben Marais, Cheryl Jones, Phil Britton, Ameneh Khatami, Alex Outhred and, most recently, as Alison and I are no longer doing on call, Annaleise Howard-Jones. Robert Booy, Cheryl Jones,

Kristine Macartney and Peter McIntyre did occasional on call work in paediatric infectious diseases. We were able to train junior doctors in paediatric infectious diseases for two years. I was the first full-time specialist paediatric infectious disease physician in Australia. Now there are paediatric infectious disease specialists in every major teaching hospital and several at the Royal Children's Hospital, Melbourne. I would like to be thought of as the Bill Marshall of Australian paediatric infectious diseases, which is ironic because Bill was an Australian who worked in London while I am a Londoner working in Australia. The youngsters call me the grandfather of Australian paediatric infectious diseases.

As a peace offering, my mother paid for a swimming pool to be built in our back garden. The children swam in summer. For nine months of the year I swam every morning for half an hour, 200 laps of an 8 metre pool. At 6am, one Autumn Friday morning it was still dark when I went for a swim. I was rolling back the pool cover while brushing away the accumulated leaves, when I felt a sharp pain in my thumb. I had bite marks and the thumb was red. I realised I must have been bitten by a funnel web spider, spiders with a venomous bite found down the East coast of Australia, and relatively common in our area. I constricted the blood supply with my other hand. My long-suffering wife drove me to the local hospital, Ryde Hospital, where a nurse applied a tourniquet. For two hours my observations were normal and it looked as if I might have got away with it. But when the nurse removed the tourniquet, I immediately started sweating profusely, drenching my clothes, and shivering uncontrollably. I developed tingling of my lips, and experienced a weird sensation as if light rain was sprinkling on my skin. Carmel gave me a drink of water, which tasted like cardboard. My blood pressure rose. The Emergency Department consultant decided to give me an injection of antivenom. He told me, reassuringly, that the side-effects of the antivenom included sudden death. Two vials of the antivenom relieved my symptoms immediately.

I was observed in their intensive care unit for a couple of hours, but my observations had returned to normal, and I was allowed home. Poor Carmel, however, had to cancel her planned spinning and weaving weekend away. My friend Henry Kilham prompted me to write an editorial about it for the JPCH (I called it *The curious incident of the bite in the night-time*) and I persuaded an expert on envenomations, Geoff Isbister, to write an accompanying commentary.

When it was too cold to swim in the pool, I walked for half an hour every day in the local park, Brush Farm, a rivulet-fed escarpment reclaimed by the council from a disused shale/mine quarry. On my walks I met Werner, who fled Germany aged 6 post–WW II, along with his single mother. Werner was passionate about native flora and fauna. He spent hours each day ridding the hillsides of non-native plants. He had a particular loathing for wandering Jew. Werner was not big on humour and I forebore pointing out to him the irony of his war on the wandering Jew. Werner was poor. He and I conceived a plan of planting Sydney blue gums. He drove me to the Cumberland State Forest nursery and I bought 40 Sydney blue gum seedlings for $100. We planted them around the forest, or rather I planted one or two under Werner's instructions, he planted the rest. Several of them are many feet tall already.

Werner knew his birds too. He told me where I might see a powerful owl nesting, the largest owl in Australia. They move nesting sites, but often return to old haunts. I looked many times and finally saw one at the site Werner had suggested. I was thrilled. Not long afterwards I went for a Sunday afternoon walk with my son Tom and his 2-year-old son Jacob. We were almost under the tree when I spotted the owl, who was looking very interested in young Jacob. A powerful owl will take a small puppy, so we kept a very close eye on Jacob.

I had not been at Westmead long when I received an email from a colleague at the University of New South Wales saying that Nigel Calvert, solicitor had emailed her asking her if she knew Dr David Isaacs. My friend Nigel Calvert had been pretty wild in his youth, but he certainly had the intellect to be a solicitor. On the other hand, this might be an unknown Nigel Calvert, solicitor acting for an unknown patient in Oxford who was suing the hospital. I had lost touch with Twiggy and was desperate to see him again. I thought that if there was a wronged patient in Oxford, then they had every right to seek redress, and I owed it to them to make that possible. I emailed Nigel Calvert, solicitor and it *was* Twiggy. He had trained as a solicitor and was hired by rock bands to look after their legal interests. I was due to visit London for a conference. Twiggy and I arranged to go to the Tate Modern and to meet at the foot of the new Millennium Bridge, just in front of the Tate Modern. I walked across the swaying bridge and waited, wondering if I would recognise Twiggy. He arrived wearing a purple velvet suit with a flower in his buttonhole, looking a tad like a character from an Oscar Wilde play. When I saw him, to my surprise, I burst into tears. He said: "Oh Little Davie", and hugged me. We saw an exhibition at the Tate Modern, then sat reminiscing in the members' café looking out over the Thames.

Since then I have kept in close touch with Twiggy. We have walked in the South Downs together and in the Cotswolds. Carmel and I visited Twiggy and his wife Gill in their terraced house in Brighton. In later years, his face has come to resemble a quizzical Rembrandt self-portrait. Twiggy blows beautiful coloured glass bowls and vases. When we were in Brighton, he offered me to choose one of the hundred or so bowls on display in his house as a gift. Carmel looked over the house first, then I did. We both chose exactly the same royal blue bowl as our favourite. When I was seriously unwell, Twiggy sent me a magnificent large, yellow bowl through the post. Every morning it looks like the sun rising. The postage must have cost a fortune. He always was such a generous man. One time he turned up at a party we were giving in London, and brought an enormous circular Stilton cheese.

Twiggy emailed me that his daughter Kate had been invited to perform at the Sydney Writers Festival. Her stage name was Kate Tempest. She was bullied at school and unhappy. She started writing poetry which she would declaim on the buses of South London, to the bewilderment of the passengers. She was the youngest ever person, at age 29, to win the Ted Hughes Award for her poem *Brand New Ancients,* which Kate performed as a spoken word poem. I asked my children if they wanted to come to the Writers Festival to listen to Kate Tempest. Anna said she knew and loved Kate Tempest's rap music and would come with me. We got there early and were in the queue when I saw Kate Tempest dressed in a white T-shirt, white jeans and white trainers. I whispered to Anna: "That's Kate Tempest". Kate turned round. "And you must be Little Divy", she said, with a broad Cockney accent. Subsequently, Kate was invited back as the main speaker of the Sydney Writers Festival. Kate has now come out as non-binary, changed name to Kae and changed pronoun to they. I find it very difficult to remember to say they. Twiggy told me he and Gill struggle too, and Kae gives them a hard time when they forget. Kae Tempest has played several times at the Glastonbury pop festival and toured the world twice with their band. Kae has published several books of poetry, has written a successful novel, and written a play *Paradise*, a modern adaptation of Sophocles' *Philoctetes,* which premiered at the National Theatre in London in 2021. Much of Kae's work is inspired by Greek writers, including *Brand New Ancients.* Tempest's song *People's Faces* was used in an uplifting Facebook commercial "We're never lost if we can find each other", which was released during the COVID-19 pandemic.

There was a global outbreak of influenza, which was called "swine flu" because it originated in pigs. When it reached Australia, there was concern when children were admitted to children's hospitals with swine flu. As a paediatric infectious diseases specialist at the main children's hospital in New South Wales, I was asked to talk to the press. The hospital's media team arranged for me to be interviewed outside the front of the hospital. To my surprise, I was expected to talk into a microphone on a stand and faced a barrage of television cameras and news reporters like a politician. I answered questions and tried to reassure the public. I was relieved when the ordeal was over. A reporter asked me if it was true that I had been infected with swine flu. I said "Yes, it's true. I caught swine flu on the dance floor at an infectious disease meeting in Brussels. Just one of life's rich little ironies." On the news that night, the newsreader said: "Paediatric infectious disease expert Professor David Isaacs says swine flu is no more serious than normal flu. And he should know." Pan to a shot of me saying: "I caught swine flu on the dance floor at an infectious disease meeting in Brussels. Just one of life's rich little ironies." This amused my medical friends no end. I thought it was funny, too, but it did teach me to beware that the camera may be rolling after an interview has supposedly ended.

When I was in Australia, I received a letter from Dr Brian Coulter from the Liverpool School of Hygiene and Tropical Medicine. He invited me to go to Kampala, Uganda for three weeks to teach young African doctors on their Masters of Medicine course. My time in Tanzania and Kenya had instilled in me a love of East Africa, the people, their colourful clothes, the landscape and the exciting atmosphere. I accepted and began to prepare enough slides and handouts to give 30 lectures. I stayed in a hostel and walked to the Mulago Hospital every day, revelling in the bright colours worn by the women and the quaint little shops, and not put off by the dust, the dogs, the continuous noise, or the wooden coffins outside the undertaker's destined mainly for the victims of HIV. The young doctors had asked for a talk on HIV infection. At that time, 30% of pregnant Ugandan women had HIV infection and half their babies developed HIV infection. I told the doctors that children with HIV infection did not suffer from the malignancy Kaposi's sarcoma which adults with HIV often get. The doctors told me I was wrong, and took me to the wards to show me children with the black gums, black roof of the mouth, and dark skin lesions characteristic of Kaposi's sarcoma. When I walked back from the hospital each afternoon, I would stop off in the market to watch the light-hearted banter as women in bright-coloured dresses bartered over the price of fruit and vegetables.

I did ward rounds with the Ugandan doctors and, although they lacked Western technology, they made up for it by being much better clinicians than most Australian and British doctors at their level. They were not paid well and I arranged to take a different doctor to lunch at the hospital cafeteria each day. It was a good way to get to know a bit about their lives.

Also staying in the hostel was a nurse called Mike. Mike walked around wearing nothing but the skimpiest of white towels round his waist. He had a pierced nipple with a metal bar through it. He was overtly gay and would ride his motorcycle to a hotel in town every night, where he would pick up other gay men. He told me he was a walking advert for condoms because he remained HIV negative despite his promiscuity.

One weekend, four of us from the hostel including Mike and I drove to the Ruwenzori Mountains ("The Mountains of the Moon") in the West of Uganda. Mike and I were sharing a room. I was a bit anxious about this and told Mike: "You do know that I'm straight, don't you Mike?" He shot back: "What makes you think I fancy you anyway." Touché.

On another occasion, a driver offered to take me to Jinja, near Lake Victoria, to see the origin of the Nile. The river flowed fiercely. Boys stood silhouetted on rocks by the river, then plunged fearlessly into the torrent in acts of bravado. I was unsure whether it was for fun, to impress me, or whether they hoped I would give them money. On the way back, the driver took me to a compound surrounded by a wicker fence. Rusted bicycles and shells of cars lay about in the compound. A man of tall stature emerged from a mud hut. He had matted dreadlocks dyed auburn, necklaces of cowrie shells, and a floor-length brown coat made of skins. He had a mystique, an aura, a presence. The driver, who was evidently in awe of him, told me I should cross his palms with silver. I did, using a silver coin which I then gave him. The man was a witch-doctor. In Tanzania, Kenya and Uganda, children coming to hospital often had recent scarification marks on their face or torso, showing they had been to see the witch-doctor before resorting to the Western doctors.

I was offered a flight on a small Royal Flying Doctor Service plane. An elderly American doctor and his wife accompanied us. We flew over fields. In one yellow field of corn, a woman was working with her red dress spread out around her, and I wishes for a camera. When we arrived at our destination deep in the jungle, the pilot approached the runway too low and fast to land. When I asked what he was doing, he said scaring the goats off the runway. He was not joking. We landed and immediately some locals appeared wearing animal skins, and surrounded by buzzing flies. The Americans asked permission to take photos. As soon as the photos were taken, the oldest man in the tribe held his hand out for money. Then all of them disappeared and came back wearing jeans and T-shirts. We stayed in a mission hospital. The pilot entertained the nuns with dirty jokes, and they roared with laughter. It seemed to be as much a social as a medical mission.

I was able to travel at weekends. I was paid quite well for my teaching. One time I decided to spend my pay on an ambitious trip to the South of Uganda, almost to the Rwandan border, to see mountain gorillas. Twelve select tourists, who had paid more than any local could afford, stayed in luxury tents in a special camp. We were split into two groups of six; each group of six would try to follow a group of about 20 mountain gorillas. The American conservationist Dian Fossey had habituated two groups of gorillas to her presence, so that they were not frightened by humans. These were the gorillas we would follow. Tragically Dian Fossey was murdered in Uganda.

Early the next morning we walked across green hillsides, our excitement mounting, until we came to a clearing overlooking the forest. A sign read: "Bwindi Impenetrable Forest". We were joined by armed guards, and the guide and guards led us down forest trails for nearly an hour. Then, on the edge of a clearing, the guide showed us a tree with the central vegetation hollowed out like a crater, and a smell of dung. "They slept here last night", he said, indicating that a large gorilla had rolled on the tree to make the hollow. "They are just across the clearing". As we crossed the clearing and neared the trees on the other side, we could see eyes peeping out of the bushes. Suddenly, we realised the eyes belonged to young gorillas watching us. The gorillas started to move through the undergrowth; we followed along a forest trail. We were as close as 15 metres from them. We were allowed to take photographs, but not use flash. We saw a huge silverback with a sore on his flank from a fight. The silverback is the alpha male. The baby gorillas bounced playfully all over him. A mother gorilla suckled her baby unconcernedly, while keeping an eye on us. It was magical. We were allowed one hour with the mountain gorillas, which passed only too quickly. We walked home in a trance. Local children sang playfully as we passed.

One week later, armed Zairean rebels stormed the very same luxury camp we had stayed in. They killed a guard and marched the tourists into the jungle towards Zaire. On the way they killed several of the tourists. They left a postcard of a silverback on one of the bodies, with a note in French. I had bought the same postcard. Luckily for me I was back in Kampala by then, but I kept visualising what it must have been like for the victims. When I returned, my friend Henry Kilham, who was an excellent cartoonist, drew a cartoon of me hugging two gorillas with the legend: "Gorillas are better than guerillas".

I loved teaching in Uganda, but I must acknowledge the strength of my wife who looked after four lively young children while I was away and never once complained. I went to Uganda three times in 10 years to teach on the Masters of Medicine course, until Brian Coulter retired.

In 1997, Kim Oates stepped down as Professor of Paediatrics at the University of Sydney and took over from John Yu as Chief Executive Officer of the Children's Hospital at Westmead. Kim asked me if I would take over his monthly visits to Bourke, and I agreed with alacrity. Firstly, Kim had always been a loyal friend, inviting us for lunches and our children swim in his pool (which he had fenced before it was mandatory). Secondly, to my chagrin, I had tried but not succeeded in nurturing links with Aboriginal communities in and around Sydney. Bourke is a small township in the "red centre" some 750 kilometres west of Sydney. There is a local expression "Back of Bourke" signifying in the middle of nowhere. Bourke's population is about 3,500, of whom around half are Aboriginal. Once a month, I would get up on a Monday at the crack of dawn to catch a 7am flight from Bankstown Airport in a tiny 6-seater Royal Flying Doctor Service Cessna (or occasionally the dreaded King Air, a much inferior plane). I would take a registrar with me and a medical student if there was room. Most trips, the plane also carried an eye specialist and an ENT specialist to Walgett. The nearest paediatricians to Bourke were in Dubbo, 370 kilometres away. The flight to Bourke took two and a half hours, and it could be turbulent especially as we flew through clouds. The pilots were highly professional and I was never scared. The only registrars who vomited were the largest, most sporting male junior doctors. The geographical patterns on the ground below often seemed to me to resemble Aboriginal paintings, perhaps a reflection of a vertical Aboriginal view of the land. One time the pilot flew us over Brewarrina, a township locals call Bree, some 96 kilometres from Bourke. Brewarrina is the site of Aboriginal fish traps: stones were placed across the Barwon River which trap fish in pools, where they can be speared or even collected with bare hands. The Brewarrina fish traps are thousands of years old and are thought to be the oldest human construction in the world.

The local general practitioners, notably Heather Dalgety, a wee Scotswoman, would refer patients, whom I would see all morning in the community clinic. The registrar would see one or two patients and discuss them with me, as a way of teaching them.

One time Heather asked me to examine her 4-year-old son, Hamish. Hamish sidled up to me and rubbed his nose on my trousers. "Oh", I said. "Are you giving me a cuddle?" "Och no", he said. "I'm wiping my boogies on your troosers". Heather was mortified, but the registrar and I thought it was hilarious.

After the morning clinic, we would have lunch at Bourke Hospital. Then the hospital staff would lend me a car. I would drive the registrar to Bourke Cemetery, for two main reasons. The great eye surgeon Fred Hollows is buried there, at his request, because he thought it was so important to treat Aboriginal eye disease. Some of the Afghan cameleers are buried there. Their mosque is made of corrugated iron, with a simple frieze of lotus flowers; it used to be in the main street but was being vandalised, so was moved to the cemetery.

We would arrive back from Bourke after 5pm. I would eat dinner and often said I was too tired to go to the weekly rehearsal of the Beecroft Orchestra. "Don't be silly, Dad," Ben would chide me. "You always say that, you always go to orchestra and you come back re-invigorated." Ben was right: I always went to the rehearsal and I never ceased to be surprised by the rejuvenative power of playing music in an ensemble.

One day Heather rang me to tell me that a one-year-old child from Brewarrina had been seen by one of the local general practitioners, and transferred to hospital but had died. The family were sad and angry. Would I speak to them. I agreed to speak to them next time I was in Bourke, and I travelled to Bree. I did not know the medical facts so I listened much more than I talked, and I stayed with them an hour. Heather told me that the family asked her afterwards if I was Aboriginal. She said that with a name like Isaacs, she doubted it. I thought it the greatest compliment they could pay me to think I might be Aboriginal. Listening is often more valuable than talking.

In 2006, I arranged to go to England for six months for a sabbatical. By then our four children were all grown up. Carmel and I flew to London and stayed for the whole six months with Stephen and Mary, which was extraordinarily generous of them. Mary, an only child, and Carmel were like sisters. Steve and I were like twin brothers as portrayed in Shakespeare's *A Comedy of Errors*: we love each other but tend to squabble. However, we almost never squabbled during the six months.

I had arranged to spend my sabbatical working in the office of Ruth Gilbert, Professor of Epidemiology at Great Ormond Street Hospital. Ruth had previously come to Oxford to get some advice from me about her research for her PhD. She was a good friend with an endearing Cockney accent. My intention, which I achieved, was to write a book on evidence-based paediatric infectious diseases. Evidence-based medicine was all the rage at that time. Before I left Sydney, I obtained invaluable advice from my Westmead colleagues Craig Mellis and Elizabeth Elliott on the best way to search for evidence.

Incidentally, I am a believer in evidence-based medicine, but it had become something of a mantra and there was some pushback about situations when it was difficult to obtain high-grade evidence. In 1999, a friend and colleague Dominic Fitzgerald and I published a satirical paper in the British Medical Journal (BMJ) called *Seven Alternatives to Evidence-Based Medicine.* In the paper we pointed out, with examples, that some people practised eminence-based medicine, some vehemence-based medicine, some eloquence-based medicine, some providence-based, some diffidence-based, some nervousness-based and some confidence-based medicine. Of all the over 500 papers I have had published, this BMJ paper is the most quoted.

Carmel explored London for six months and was not bored for a minute. I was reminded of what Samuel Johnson wrote in the 18th century: "When a man is tired of London, he is tired of life" (women counted for very little in the 18th century). Carmel and I would go for walks on Hampstead Heath with Ruth, her husband Jan and their boys, Max and Joe. I attended Grand Rounds at Great Ormond Street every week. I was disappointed that they were so poorly attended, but delighted to see the luminary Otto Woolf, tall with white hair, who attended every week. Ruth cried when we left. I was touched and had a lump in my throat, too. Steve and Mary must have been relieved to have their house back to themselves, but they did not show it.

Bill Marshall did a lot of teaching in Malaysia. I, too, made several trips to Malaysia, teaching or giving invited lectures. On the first trip, I taught on a course in Kota Bharu, Kelantan Province in the North. One memorable weekend I travelled with two young Malaysian doctors to Perhentian Island. The tourist season had ended and the men working in the empty café said there were no snorkels to be had. But one of the young doctors told them I was an Underwater Professor. Snorkels and flippers miraculously appeared and we were able to watch brilliantly coloured fish in the reef just off the shore. The island was almost deserted. We slept in little wicker cabins. In the morning I woke to a mewing noise, to find it came from sea-eagles floating majestically overhead. The empty beach was fringed by palm-trees. This is paradise, I thought to myself. We explored the small island. On one beach, a woman was usiing a chopper to hack open a coconut to feed a small child. Fishermen tended to their boat and nets.

In Kota Bharu, the paediatrician, Dr Choo, told me that there was discrimination against the Chinese in Malaysia. Dr Choo loved old black-and-white films, so I used to bring him videotapes of those films when I came for further visits. I gave frequent talks in Kuala Lumpur, and became close friends with Wan Ariffin, an oncologist whom I had originally met when we were both working at Queen Elizabeth, Hackney. Wan Ariffin, a Malay national, is an ardent Bob Dylan fan and had T-shirts to prove it. I also became friends with Jessie de Bruyne, a Malay respiratory physician who did some of her studies in Sheffield. She had something of a North England accent. One trip, I brought the first of the Harry Potter books for her children. She told me they were already onto Book Three. Harry Potter had already made it to Malaysia. I sometimes wondered if I was trying to emulate Bill Marshall, but I think we both independently came to love Malaysia and its people.

The other place I worked a few times was in Port Moresby, Papua New Guinea. The Professor of Paediatrics, John Vince, was English, married to a local Papuan woman. John invited me to examine candidates on their Masters of Medicine course. Port Moresby was a dangerous place. We were told not to leave the compound where we were housed. Foolishly, I walked to the local market one day, with my camera prominently round my neck. I was the only white person there, I was followed back to the compound and was lucky not to be mugged. People kept their car doors locked when driving and did not stop at red lights for fear of being attacked by men with guns. Armed men attacked John Vince's house one day. John's teenage son came out shouting and wielding a hockey-stick, and the men ran away. His father was proud of his courage, but relieved he didn't get shot.

I always liked writing and had a secret ambition to emulate my mentor, Bernie Valman, who was Editor-in-Chief of the British paediatric journal Archives of Disease in Childhood. I was appointed to the editorial board of the Australasian paediatric journal, the Journal of Paediatrics and Child Health (JPCH). When Frank Oberklaid, the Editor-in-Chief of the JPCH, stepped down, I decided to apply for the position. I was offered an interview and Peter Procopis told me to bring a list of 5 Key Objectives to the interview. I asked why, if I was the only applicant for an onerous, unpaid position. He told me to stop complaining and bring the Objectives. At the interview, Peter had also written his 5 Key Objectives for the journal. We compared them; they were identical.

I loved being Editor-in-Chief of the Journal of Paediatrics and Child Health. One of the Objectives was to brighten up the journal. We did this by sourcing artworks and photographs by children, those who contributed to Joanna Capon's Art Express but also children's art competitions run by the Art Department in our hospital. Wiley-Blackwell added colour to what had previously been a black-and-white journal. I decided to write editorials every month on varied topics relevant to paediatrics and paediatricians. I used a photograph to accompany each of my editorials. My friend and deputy Editor-in-Chief, Mike South educated me that I could use any photograph in *Wikimedia Commons: Images* without infringing copyright. That was a Godsend. I was Editor-in-Chief for 14 years until forced to step down by illness, so I wrote over 150 editorials. My first editorial in 2009 was to thank the previous Editor-in-Chief, Frank Oberklaid (although I still regret pointing out that his secret nickname was Frankly Overpaid). My second was on "Humour in Paediatrics". The last in 2023 was on "Control and Stoicism". With great kindness and generosity, our social media editor Chris Elliot had all my editorials bound in a book as a gift when I was no longer Editor-in-Chief.

My good friend the late Henry Kilham was a prolific cartoonist, and I was able to use several of his best cartoons in the journal. I don't remember all of the Objectives, but we more than doubled the Impact Factor, a measure of how often a journal's papers are referred to by other journals. Improving the Impact Factor was certainly one of the 5 Key Objectives.

I have published widely, over 500 peer-reviewed papers and 10 medical textbooks, but I never really considered myself a researcher like my colleagues William Tarnow-Mordi, Ben Marais, David Burgner and Phil Britton. I was just a clinician who was interested in children and their infectious diseases. As a 9-year-old I had wanted to be a Professor. Kim Oates pushed me to apply to be a Clinical Professor and advised me on the content needed for a strong application. I was paid by the hospital so it didn't cost the University of Sydney a cent to make me Clinical Professor in Paediatric Infectious Diseases, which they did. Not long afterwards, I was walking down the corridor when I met the Professor of Medicine, Kim Oates, and the Professor of Surgery, Douglas Cohen. Kim put an arm around my shoulder and said: "Have you heard that this young man has just been made into a Professor?" "Harrumph, they're just like arseholes. Everyone's got one", said Douglas Cohen. The young doctors thought it was disrespectful to call me David (or Little Davie) so they all called me Prof. Being called "Prof" gives me an inner glow.

The Prickly Pair

In my family folk history, I was the musician and my identical twin brother Stephen was the artist. That folk history always seemed to me a bit contrived: a self-fulfilling prophecy. I was a very average second violinist, but loved playing in The Beecroft Orchestra, our local orchestra, under our revered conductor Joanna Drimatis. Steve attended weekly art classes and painted some high class paintings. My favourite is one of Vincent van Gogh he gave Carmel and me as a gift. Stephen and I wrote three children's books. He did all the art works and we shared the writing. Our first book, *The Prickly Pair*, is about twin porcupines and is set in Tuscany. The second, *Ouch in the Pouch*, is about marsupials and monotremes. The third is about dinosaurs. The royalties will not make us rich.

One Christmas my grown-up children gave me some ceramics lessons. I cannot compare to Stephen as an artist, but

I loved decorating pre-made ceramics under the tutelage of Yu Mi, a lovely Japanese teacher. I renewed my lessons and continued making ceramic plates and jugs for some years until forced to stop by illness. There is something uplifting about being creative; that creativity can take a number of forms, but it is always worth being open-minded.

One day when I was in my late sixties, they were offering to measure anyone's blood pressure in the outpatients department. I had mine measured and it was sky-high, 205/130. I saw my general practitioner (GP) urgently. That evening I rang my twin brother Stephen in London to tell him my news, only for him to tell me he had been newly diagnosed with high blood pressure that same day, 11,000 miles away. He told me his blood pressure was 170/100. "Mine's much higher," I said. "Well you are ten minutes older," he shot back. A great line. I know we are identical twins, but that degree of concordance seems quite extraordinary to me.

In 2005, the United Nations asked countries like Australia, which takes a few thousand refugees every year, to prioritise refugees from Burundi. Our adult infectious disease colleagues at Westmead Hospital found that, even though the Burundi patients coming to their clinic were well, a number of them had malaria parasites seen in their blood films. In Africa, many people live with malaria parasites in their bloodstream, but their immune system holds the parasites in check. The concern was that, when away from Africa, their immunity might wane and they might get clinical malaria. Our adult colleagues asked us to see the Burundi children in their clinic, which we did for a while. However, we realised that what we needed was a clinic to see the child refugees from Burundi and from other countries. My friend David Burgner had been running a Refugee Clinic in Perth for years, which convinced me of the need. My colleague Nick Wood and I made a financial case for a clinic coordinator and social work support. We opened the HARK (Health Assessment for Refugee Kids) Clinic in 2005. The coordinator and the social worker were salaried, but all the HARK doctors volunteered their time, notably a University of Sydney employee Hasantha Gunasekera (Has). Merran Mackenzie and Helen Young. The initial aim of the HARK Clinic was to screen refugee children for treatable conditions, mostly infections such as tuberculosis and hepatitis B, but also anaemia (sometimes due to sickle cell anaemia in African children) and rickets. We also planned to immunise any children who had not been immunised. However, with time we came to realise that many of the families we saw had fled war-torn areas and were victims of or had witnessed physical and/or sexual violence. Furthermore there were some countries, such as Afghanistan, where people fleeing violence, fearful for their lives, had no access to a United Nations office to register as a refugee. These people fled in boats or planes and were deemed to be seeking asylum.

At HARK, Has and I saw both refugees and people seeking asylum. Dr Helen Young, a paediatric neurologist and general paediatrician, joined HARK after a mother and child were transferred to her hospital, Royal North Shore Hospital. Helen cared for the infant and sought our help in her battle to ensure the child and her family were not sent back to Nauru. Dr Merran Mackenzie (a GP) and Dr Jennifer Anderson also joined the HARK team. Alanna Maycock was Clinic Coordinator and Zoe Bell and then Selina Oum were social workers. When Alanna was promoted to Clinical Nurse Consultant (CNC), Nadine Shema, a Rwandan doctor, was employed as Coordinator. The current Head of HARK is Nicola Morton, who also works for Médecins sans Frontières (Doctors without Borders). Kylie McNulty is the new CNC, succeeding Alanna. The Australian Government classed people arriving seeking asylum as illegal immigrants, particularly when they came by boat, not when they came by plane. Cynics suggested white Australians were scared of people arriving by boat because the first white people to colonise Australia arrived by boat in 1788 as the First Fleet, then stole the land from Aborigines. Aboriginal people had been living in Australia for over 60,000 years.

David and Steve

CHAPTER FOURTEEN: NAURU AND THE ACCIDENTAL ACTIVIST

Many boats carrying people seeking asylum to Australia, particularly those coming from Indonesia, arrived at Christmas Island, an Australian territory in the Indian Ocean. The 1951 Refugee Convention, to which Australia is a signatory, says that a person fleeing persecution in fear of their life cannot be transferred to another country. Australia overcame their moral obligations by cynically excising Christmas Island from mainland Australia, just as the United States excised Guantanamo Bay from the USA so they could hold prisoners there indefinitely without trial. When people arrived in boats at Christmas Island and asked for asylum, Australia held some in a detention centre on Christmas Island and flew others to the tiny Pacific island republic of Nauru or to Manus Island in Papua New Guinea.

In 2012, aged 24, our youngest son Mark graduated with a BA degree in international studies and communication from the University of Technology Sydney (UTS) and was working in a government position that did not excite him. A friend told him that the Salvation Army was hiring humanitarian workers to look after the men (it was only adult men then) held in immigration detention on Nauru. Mark rang the Salvation Army who were obviously desperate because they hired him over the phone without an interview, without asking for referees, and with no character check. They even asked him if he could fly the next day. Mark flew to Nauru a week later. He was horrified by what he saw. The men were in a detention centre that looked like a concentration camp, with spotlights, fences, barbed wire and massive guards. The detained men asked him when they would be released; he had no answer. Their detention was indefinite. They pointed out to him that common criminals at least know their release date; they can look forward to the day they will be released. The men on Nauru did not know if they would ever be released. Mark did his best to make life more bearable for the men. He organised a cricket tournament, a soccer tournament, and trips to the beach (where he bought all the men ice-creams). He befriended many of the men. But, as they pointed out to him, Mark could go back to his family for two weeks after every four week shift. They were unable to see their family. And they had done nothing wrong, except flee from persecution to try to give their family a better life.

Mark kept a diary. His contract with the Salvation Army forbade him from describing what was happening on Nauru, even on social media. After nine months on Nauru, Mark decided he needed to resign from the Salvation Army, so he could try to shine a light on the horrors of the immigration detention system. He transformed his diary into a book, which was published by Hardie Grant as *The Undesirables: Inside Nauru*. The book received a highly favourable review from author Thomas Keneally, who called Mark "a bewildered pilgrim." Mark was interviewed by journalist Sarah Ferguson at the Sydney Writers Festival in front of a full house. He was only 26 years old. He became an activist for refugees and people seeking asylum. Mark has just been awarded his PhD on people smugglers: in World War II people who smuggled Jews away from the Nazis were heroes. Now we demonise people smugglers as evil. Mark's thesis interrogates political narratives about people smuggling and exposes the Australian government's use of extrajudicial administrative punishments on suspected people smugglers. I am very proud of Mark's stand against injustice. But then I'm very proud of all my children.

In 2014, two years after Mark had been on Nauru, I was asked by International Health and Medical Services (IHMS) if I would fly to Nauru for five days to consult on children in immigration detention. Originally men, women and children had been sent to Manus Island in Papua New Guinea, but the children were at high risk of malaria on Manus. Therefore, women and children were transferred to Nauru. IHMS is a private organisation to which the Australian government pays exorbitant amounts of money to outsource the provision of health services to people in immigration detention. There were emergency medicine specialists and general practitioners on Nauru, but no other specialists. Therefore, IHMS would recruit specialists to be flown in every few months, a costly and inefficient way of providing specialist health care. I agonised about the ethics of going to Nauru. Was I being complicit with the harms that were being done to those in immigration detention by the Australian government? On the positive side, I would be able to give an eye witness account of what life was like for those on Nauru. I agreed to go to Nauru, on two conditions. The first was that IHMS fly our HARK Clinical Nurse Consultant, Alanna Maycock, out with me. The second was that Alanna and I would be allowed to visit the living quarters, something that had been denied our HARK colleague Has Gunasekera when he went to Nauru for IHMS 3 months earlier. Alanna and I had to sign contracts saying we would not disclose anything detrimental to the Government or IHMS about Nauru. Alanna and I were very well paid and decided we would donate all our earnings to the HARK Clinic; the thought that the federal Government would be sponsoring HARK via IHMS amused us.

Nauru is a tiny island, four hours' flying time from Brisbane. As the plane approaches, the island is scarcely more than a flat speck on the ocean. The men seeking asylum told Mark that as they landed they thought they were about to land in the sea. The periphery of the island is studded with palm trees; the gleaming ocean and offshore reef gives every sign of an idyllic Pacific island. Immediately inland, however, the land is bare of grass and trees and is pockmarked with the remnants of phosphate mining. Australia colonised Nauru, "collaborated" with Nauru to harvest all its phosphate, then left the Nauruans to clean up the mess. The devastated landscape and broken machinery shows the mess is yet to be cleaned up. Visiting dignitaries and politicians stay in a hotel on the coast, cooled by sea breezes. People in immigration detention stay in guarded detention centres on the hottest part of the island.

I can honestly say that Alanna and I were in shock at what we saw. The people in the detention centre lived in rows of tents, all adjacent to each other. Guards would sometimes push the tent flap aside without warning. There was no privacy. The block housing the toilets and showers was 30 to 120 metres distant from the living quarters. Many women and children wet the bed at night rather than face the night-time walk to the toilets under the scrutiny of massive Nauruan guards. One distraught woman wept bitterly as she told me she had been raped by a guard, but did not want to make an official complaint because she did not want her husband to know. Sanitary arrangements for women were totally inadequate; Alanna brought sanitary pads in her luggage having been told of the problem, but it was a band-aid solution to an ongoing problem. Showers were limited to two minutes, supposedly because of water shortage, but the guards would offer women longer showers if they would open the shower curtain to expose themselves.

When we saw children in the medical clinic, the nurses called for them by their boat number, not their name, however much we protested that this dehumanised them. I saw about 30 children in five days. All the parents were clinically depressed. They were in despair that they had fled persecution to give their children a better life, only to find themselves in a worse position, imprisoned without trial or right of appeal, uncertain if they would ever be released. Parents in that sort of state have great difficulty setting limits for their children; many of the children consequently had behavioural problems. We saw a six-year-old girl with strangulation marks round her neck from trying to harm herself with a fence tie. We saw a 15-year-old who had sewn his lips together to protest against the situation and was refusing food and drink, until his parents allowed the doctor to cut the ties to save his life. All the families cried when telling me their stories; so did I, and the interpreters often cried too. Years later I saw a man who had been an interpreter on Nauru. He said: "I remember you. You're the doctor who cries with his patients". Only on Nauru, I thought. After a short while, I told every family two things. Firstly, there are many people back in Australia like us who do not agree with what our Government is doing to you. Secondly, I promise to do everything I can to let the Australian public know the awful conditions under which you are living.

After five days, Alanna and I were shattered. How did Mark manage 9 months? And how much worse for the detainees themselves. When Alanna and I returned to Sydney, we composed an opinion piece for the newspaper. I was a bit concerned about the restrictive contract we had signed with IHMS. My son Mark put me in touch with the human rights lawyer Julian Burnside. Mark met Julian on Nauru when Julian was trying unsuccessfully to get the detainees released, arguing that they were prisoners being held without trial. Julian read our piece, said it was strong, and that we would not be breaking our contract if we were "exposing iniquity" Clearly, he said, what was being done on Nauru constituted iniquity. Our opinion piece was published in The Sydney Morning Herald and The Age. IHMS were angry with us, but took it no further. We would never be invited back to Nauru by IHMS, but we still had to work with IHMS for people in community detention in Sydney who attended our HARK Clinic.

Alanna and I acquired a reputation. I talked at mass rallies. Using a megaphone to talk to a crowd in front of Sydney Town Hall was a far cry from talking to a scientific audience. We marched with vast crowds at protest rallies. Medical students asked us to march with them. Film-maker Heather Kirkpatrick made a film *Against Our Oath*, in which we featured, which argued that doctors working with people in immigration detention were contravening the Hippocratic oath. Alanna was invited to the Women in the World conference in New York. She gave a talk just after the Scottish Prime Minister, Nicola Sturgeon and just before Hilary Clinton.

In 2015, the Australian government inexplicably passed a law, the *Australian Border Force Bill 2015*, which stated that anyone under contract with the government or its contracted partners (including IHMS) who revealed what was happening in detention centres faced up to two years' imprisonment. The law applied to teachers, social workers and lawyers as well as doctors and nurses. Two years in prison for telling the truth. The law did not specify if it could be applied retrospectively or only prospectively. I wrote an open letter to the Prime Minister, Malcolm Turnbull, asking him to prosecute me, and sent a copy to the newspapers, which they published. My colleagues at work asked me if I was going to prison. I was pretty sure the Government would not take me on, and I had the reassurance that if they did prosecute me, Julian Burnside had promised to defend me free of charge. My children had grown up, so if they did send me to prison I would have more time to write editorials. I am not by nature a political person but, in advocating for children mistreated by the government, I had become an accidental activist.

Because of our shared stand against the Australian Government's imprisonment of asylum seekers and refugees offshore, I became friends with Gillian Triggs, a distinguished human rights lawyer who was President of the Australian Human Rights Commission from 2012 to 2017. Alanna, Has, Helen and I met her at the AHRC, and she invited Alanna and me to a party at our house. She published a book *Speaking Up* at the same time as my book *Defeating the Ministers of Death* and Mark's book *The Peace Hosue of Kabul* were published. All 3 of us were invited to the Brisbane Writers Festival and I took Gillian Triggs out to dinner, together with Mark, an ethicist friend Melanie Jansen, and my sister-in-law Gina and her daughter Olivia.

In February 2018 there were still 158 children on Nauru; all of them had been there more than five years. Some children seeking asylum had spent their whole lives on Nauru, Some children and their families were accepted to be re-settled in the United States, but not those who originally came from Iran or Afghanistan. One by one, the children remaining on Nauru started to develop what is called pervasive refusal syndrome. The children would take to their bed, turn their face to the wall and refuse to eat or drink. They would not talk and would not wash. Some wet or soiled the bed. Refusal to drink on a tropical island is incompatible with survival for more than a couple of days. If a parent took their child to the Republic of Nauru Hospital because the child was refusing to drink, the parent was threatened that if they did not make their child drink, the staff would call the police to have the parent arrested. Refugee activists started to hear about these children; they contacted lawyers to act for the family *pro bono*. The lawyers needed evidence, so contacted those of us working at HARK. Alanna worked tirelessly and selflessly. She arranged video consultations with the family and she arranged for an interpreter for each consultation. Alanna lived over an hour's drive from the hospital, yet she would organise for a video consultation at 7am before the weekly HARK meeting, and often another one at 5pm after HARK. Alanna would contact the families on Nauru using her smart phone. A doctor, Hasantha Gunasekera, Helen Young or I, would interview the family through an interpreter. Then the parents would use their phone to show us the child's appearance. The doctor who did the interview would write a letter to the lawyer, stating that the child had the following features consistent with a diagnosis of pervasive refusal syndrome, that their life was in danger, and that they needed to be transferred to Australia immediately for medical care. The lawyer would approach the Department of Immigration asking for an immediate transfer. The government would oppose the transfer until the case was about to go to Court, then the government would back down. The government backed down because if the case hadn't been to Court, it wouldn't be reported by the Press.

This was desperate stuff. I lived in fear that a child would die. At least one child had to go to intensive care when they arrived in Australia. We looked after one child with severe pervasive refusal syndrome at The Children's Hospital at Westmead. She had refused to drink from Nauru through

Brisbane to Sydney, and would not take a sip of water from me. We had to persuade her to let us put a tube down her nose into her stomach (a nasogastric tube) to give her fluids for her first week with us. She stayed in hospital three months until she was well enough to live in the community. She used to chide the security guards for tormenting a child. She is an incredibly brave young person, but has been damaged, perhaps for ever, by what she has suffered.

In 2018, World Vision mounted a campaign #KidsOffNauru, which had support from many charitable organisations. My son Mark and I were both ambassadors for #KidsOffNauru. It was remarkable to see how public opinion changed. In 2017, 60% of Australians surveyed felt the government's immigration policy was OK or not harsh enough. By October 2018, 79% of Australians wanted all children off Nauru. The government was forced by public opinion to acquiesce. By the end of 2018, all children on Nauru had been transferred to Australia. In less than a year, over 150 children had been rescued from detention, having spent over five years on Nauru. The government had the gall to boast about getting the children off Nauru. We decided our role at HARK was to help these children recover from the traumas they had experienced and to get their life back on track.

Independent film-maker Heather Kirkpatrick from Tasmania made an award-winning documentary film, *Mary Meets Mohammad*, about an elderly woman who befriends a refugee. Heather approached me amongst others when she was making a film, *Against Our Oath*, arguing that immigration legislation was causing doctors to act in violation of the Hippocratic Oath. Heather filmed me at home and, with permission, at the Children's Hospital at Westmead, examining a child (for privacy reasons I was examining Phil Britton's son, Sam). The première at a cinema in Randwick was a memorable occasion. Heather has become a close friend.

I have often been asked if my advocacy of refugees and people seeking asylum has adversely affected my career. There is only one instance that I know of. For 8 proud years I was a member of the Pharmaceutical Benefits Advisory Committee (PBAC), which advises the government whether drugs and vaccines are cost-effective and can be considered for the Pharmaceutical Benefits Scheme (PBS) or which vaccines could be considered for the routine immunisation schedule. The nearest equivalent to the PBAC is NICE (the National Institute for health and Clinical Excellence) in the United Kingdom, which advises the National Health Service on whether drugs are cost-effective. It is an effective way of limiting the cost of drugs and vaccines to the nation. I loved being on the PBAC. It was hard work: three 3-day meetings a year and 40 hours' preparation reading the paperwork for each meeting. But we all bonded together. The Secretary of the PBAC, Di McDonell, told me that she and her husband Brian met at a "Come as bare as you dare" party. She and Brian were fully clad, but they were shocked that some people just wore tinsel. Di was English, of course. I giggled at Di's horror.

There were about 30 members of the PBAC and two community appointees. Barry was a senior community appointment. One day, after lunch, Barry fell fast asleep, his head back, his mouth open. I sent a text message saying: "I think Barry has just died". The message was passed around the committee to snorts of suppressed laughter. Only the puzzled PBAC Chair, Lloyd Sansom, the Secretary Di McDonell, and Barry, still asleep, did not know what was going on. It was a bit puerile of me, but the meetings were so intense, a bit of levity was welcome.

After I had completed my 8 year term on the PBAC, I continued to chair the Nutritional Products Working Party which advised the PBAC on products such as infant formulas. Children with rare inborn errors of metabolism may be helped by enzymes to replace those they are missing, but typically these enzymes are very expensive, in the order of $300,000 per child per year. The government, therefore, created a Life-Saving Drugs Programme; something over 200 children receive enzyme replacement therapy through this programme. The PBAC administered the Life-Saving Drugs Programme, until it was realised that the PBAC was for cost-effective drugs and vaccines, whereas the enzymes were not cost-effective. The Department of Health decided to create a Committee which would consider high cost drugs that were not cost-effective. These were mainly for children. I received a phone call from the Department of Health asking me to chair this Committee. I asked what it would entail. I was ambivalent, but decided that it was addressing an important problem, so agreed to chair the Committee. I heard nothing for a while. Then I received a phone call from the Department of Health telling me that my application to be a member of the Committee had been unsuccessful. Puzzled, I said, "But you asked me to *chair* the Committee." "There must have been some sort of misunderstanding." The penny dropped. "This wouldn't have anything to do with my support of refugees, would it?" I asked. There was an immediate, "Oh no. Nothing like that". I found out later that the Minister of Health put my name forward to Cabinet to chair the Committee, but my name was vetoed by two members of Cabinet. It would not surprise me if the two were Peter Dutton and Scott Morrison, both of whom I had corresponded with when they had been Minister for Immigration. My friends told me to wear my rejection as a Badge of Pride, which I do.

Documentary feature film available at againstouroath.com

CHAPTER FIFTEEN: CLINICAL ETHICS

Henry Kilham and I both had a long-standing interest in clinical ethics, not the Research Ethics Committee which considers whether or not research studies are ethical, but the ethics of everyday clinical work in a children's hospital. Henry enrolled to do a Masters course in Bioethics as an external post-graduate degree at Monash University, Melbourne. Inspired by Henry, I enrolled for the same course. The Masters course necessitated spending 10 hours a week reading and essay-writing, on top of our existing clinical load. That may not sound excessive, but if we had a busy week on call and were too tired to read and write ethics, that was 20 hours extra work the next week. It was fascinating but challenging to have to read the often dense writing of ethicists and philosophers and to have to write academic essays for the first time since university. Henry and I enjoyed discussing topics and comparing each other's essays. One unexpected effect of the bioethics course was that I became pescatarian. I had become increasingly concerned by the practice of feeding antibiotics to animals merely to increase yield, not for the animals' sake, and by the practice of feeding sheep offal to cows, for economic reasons, which resulted in mad cow disease. We studied the writing of Peter Singer, who is a strict vegetarian, and makes a strong case for vegetarianism. I promptly became a vegetarian.

Henry and I both did a one-week intensive course, organised by Monash University, at Mount Buller. There were lectures all morning and late in the evenings, which were of high quality. But the highlight of the week for me was the free afternoons when we would go on bracing walks in the Victorian Alps and talk to each other in depth. Helga Kuhse, the distinguished ethicist who worked with and published books with Peter Singer, went on those walks. It was fascinating talking to her, if you could keep up with her. She struck a vigorous pace.

After two years of Clinical Ethics, Henry and I both acquired a Postgraduate Diploma in Bioethics. We were too exhausted to face writing a long thesis for a Masters degree. Armed with our qualifications, we started the first ever Clinical Ethics service at The Children's Hospital at Westmead. We offered our colleagues ethics consultations in situations that were ethically complex. We arranged to give Clinical Ethics Grand Rounds presentations three times a year, with Bernadette Tobin from St Vincent's Hospital as a visiting ethicist to provide an expert commentary on the cases presented. Clinical Ethics Grand Rounds soon became the best attended of all Grand Rounds. Henry and I also arranged monthly Clinical Ethics meetings where we or a colleague would present a child whose management was causing ethical problems, then open up the case for general discussion.

When we could, Henry and I would attend meetings at the Centre for Values, Ethics and the Law in Medicine (VELIM) of the University of Sydney. VELIM was started by the Professor of Surgery at Westmead Hospital, the late Miles Little. Miles was a humanist and a poet as well as a surgeon. He was widely read in philosophy and bioethics. He was succeeded by Professor Ian Kerridge and later by Professor Angus Dawson. Henry and I taught on the Masters of Bioethics course for the University of Sydney and I co-supervised a successful PhD student.

Henry and I had clinical demands on our time competing with clinical ethics. Henry made a strong case for the Sydney Children's Hospital Network (The Children's Hospital at Westmead and Sydney Children's Hospital, Randwick) to fund a full-time ethicist. Eventually the hospital paid attention. Anne Preisz was appointed as Clinical Ethicist and is now Lead for the Clinical Ethics Support Service. She works across two hospitals, and is extremely busy. Henry and I worked with her as clinician–ethicists until we retired.

Associate Professor Phil Britton is now the lead clinician supporting Anne. Anne has succeeded in persuading the Network to fund a Fellow in Clinical Ethics to help cope with the burgeoning demand for ethical advice. One of Anne's stellar achievements is to develop a matrix to help staff cope with aggressive parents, something which sadly seems to be an increasing problem.

Mark presents on David at the Global Health Conference 2019

CHAPTER SIXTEEN: HEALTH MATTERS

Our eldest child, Anna, took an Arts degree with Psychology at Macquarie University, Sydney. She wanted to specialise in Psychology, but was told she would need an average of B's in her first year to be allowed to do Psychology. She got an average of A's and specialised in Psychology. At the end of her third year, Anna received the vice chancellor's award for academic excellence. Her teachers wanted her to do a PhD, but Anna had decided to study medicine. She worked for a year on a project about bowel cancer screening in the Department of Public Health at the University of Sydney. She studied hard, passed the entrance examination to medicine (the GAMSAT) and the viva, and was accepted to study medicine at the University of Sydney. After completing her medical student studies, Anna decided to become a surgeon. She said to me: "Do you know what you said when I said I was going to be a surgeon?" "What?" "You said: 'Oh no, so you're not going to be part of the caring profession.'" "*Moi*?" "Yes, you Dad". Truth is, of course, I am immensely proud of Anna's achievements. She accomplished a long and arduous training programme to become a specialist in upper gastro-intestinal surgery, now works at Tweed Heads Hospital and John Flynn Hospital and lives on the Gold Coast. She achieved this while she and her wonderful partner, Peter, and Peter's parents raised a son, Charlie, now aged 10 and a daughter, Zoe, aged 4.

Our third child, Tom, obtained a BA in Fine Arts at the University of Sydney. He then became a performance artist, and also graduated as a child care worker. Tom gained a PhD in Fine Arts from the University of Sydney for his thesis on the relationship between performance art and ritual. Tom called one of his performances *Shiva*; in it he uncovers mirrors, which is part of the Shiva ritual. Obviously this was a reference to what happened to his grandfather Alick. In 2024, Tom gave an invited artist's talk at the Art Gallery of New South Wales on Louise Bourgeois and psychoanalysis. The talk was given during the Louise Bourgeois exhibition hosted by the Gallery. Carmel, Anna and I attended the talk and were bursting with pride. Tom and his wife, Cathrine, have a 6-year-old son Jacob. Needless to say, I am exceedingly proud of Tom and his considerable achievements.

Mark, our fourth and youngest child, was called Golden Balls by his siblings because, no matter what he did, he seemed to come up trumps and the sun shone out of his backside. He and his wife Tika (Kartika in full) have two boys, Tanah aged 4 (Tanah means the soil, the earth in Indonesian) and Asri aged one (Asri means lush vegetation in Indonesian). Tika has Indonesian parents, was raised in Australia and is bilingual. She has a senior management role in Uber. In 2024, Mark was awarded his PhD on people smugglers. He is a journalist and has started writing his fourth book. Mark wrote two other books after *The Undesirables. Nauru Burning: The Story* is about a riot that took place on Nauru and the vicious, even murderous response of some guards. *The Kabul Peace House* is an uplifting account of a house in Kabul run by a doctor, who brought together Afghans who were traditional enemies and taught them to live in harmony. Mark lived with them in Kabul for some weeks interviewing members of the Peace House. When the Taliban returned, the members of the peace house fled, but Mark kept in touch with them. When Mark was invited to speak at the Berlin Writers Festival, Mark arranged that two Afghan members of the Peace House who had fled to Germany spoke with him. Mark, Tika, Tanah and Asri live in Ocean Shores, near Byron Bay.

Our second child, Ben, was extremely bright. He was an avid reader. The sports teacher commented that Ben might have been quite good at hockey if he didn't hold a book in one hand while playing. He went to Eastwood Primary School and qualified for James Ruse Agricultural College, the most difficult of all the selective schools to reach. Ben was an anxious boy and we pondered whether he would be better at James Ruse or at a state school. We thought, rightly, that Ben might meet like-minded boys ("geeks") at James Ruse. Ben never did his homework. The school would ring me to tell me, and ask me what I was going to do about it. I would say: "But I did not set the homework. You did. It is up to you to come up with the consequences." I didn't want to fight with Ben over it. I would sometimes ask Ben if he didn't think he should do more work. "Would you rather I came bottom at James Ruse or top at the state school?" I would say: "Well ..." He would say: "Shut up, Dad".

Ben did just fine at James Ruse. He made friends, he gained a place at Macquarie University to study English, and succeeded in obtaining a BA in English. Ben was a bit rudderless after university. He worked in a cinema and at the Sydney Aquarium in poorly paid jobs and lived at home. Carmel said to Ben that he had enjoyed working in the library doing work experience. If he would go to TAFE (a college of further education) to study to be a librarian, she would pay him what he would have earned at the aquarium. Ben breezed his way through the TAFE course and was able to get a job at Macquarie University Library as an assistant librarian. Ben worked extremely hard and was soon promoted to a full librarian. He enjoyed helping the students and was very popular with them. He was always popular with his colleagues, too. Ben moved into a shared flat with two friends. He and his many friends were happiest playing computer games and board games together, sometimes all night.

In 2017, Ben went to his general practitioner because a spot on his back kept bleeding. The GP thought it was an innocent lesion but, to be careful, snipped it off and sent it for histology. The histology showed malignant melanoma, the disease that killed Bob Marley. Ben faced a barrage of investigations, which showed that the melanoma had spread to his lymph nodes. Ben had radiotherapy to his back, which gave him burns, and chemotherapy. Novel treatments for melanoma include agents that stimulate the patient's immune system to recognise the melanoma cells as foreign. However, the agents can also cause the patient to have auto-immune reactions (reactions against the patient's own tissues). When he was taking one of the novel agents for bone secondaries, Ben developed life-threatening hepatitis, which put him in hospital for a few days and prevented him having the agent again.

Ben's response to having a malignancy that would likely prove fatal was to say: "It is what it is." I think this was his way of shutting off further consideration of the topic, to avoid making him more anxious. Ben's brothers Tom and Mark wanted to talk to Ben about his feelings. I asked a palliative care physician friend, Linda Sheahan, if she would talk to them. She kindly agreed and both Tom and Mark spoke to her on the phone. Linda told them that people reacted very differently to a diagnosis of a probable terminal illness. She said that Ben was an adult and, if he preferred not to talk about his illness, presumably because it made him more anxious to do so, then surely we owed it to him to respect his wishes. Tom and Mark could accept Linda's counsel and stopped worrying so much about getting Ben to express his feelings.

Ben's melanoma progressed inexorably over six years. He developed a lesion in his brain. The neurosurgeon proposed to biopsy it to make sure it was melanoma and not something else such as an infection. Before the surgery, Ben gave Carmel the PIN for his phone. He was fearful that his brain would be damaged by the surgery and he would forget his PIN. The operation went well. Ben woke bright and chirpy, fully conscious, and immediately knew his PIN without prompting. The brain lesion was a secondary melanoma.

Anna elected to do 9 months of her specialist upper gastro-intestinal surgery training at Concord Hospital in Sydney, so that she could be close to Ben. Ben's care was through Westmead Hospital and Anna had done her early surgical training at Westmead Hospital, including some melanoma surgery. Carmel helped Anna and Peter find a rental house just 150 metres from Ben's apartment. Peter is a superb cook and Ben was invited for dinner most evenings. Sometimes Ben could walk the 150 metres, but often he was too exhausted and needed a lift. When he arrived, Zoe would bring a book and Ben would always find the strength to read to Zoe.

Ben had three melanoma deposits in his bowel. They bled silently and Ben became anaemic. He needed a blood transfusion every 3–4 weeks. Ben's dearest wish was to go to England to spend some time with his belovèd cousin, Catherine, her husband Tom W. and their children Owen and Sophia. He also wanted to see his cousin Emily and her husband Dave, and his cousin Jonni and his husband Tim. Ben had always kept in contact with Catherine, ever since they were cousins living nearby in Finchley. Ben's oncologist said there was a window for him to go to London, but he also said to Ben: "You do know that you might never come back, don't you?" Ben said he knew. Ben and I flew together. He was so tired that I had to push him in a wheelchair at the airport in Sydney, Singapore and London. Ben did not like being dependent, and was a bit tetchy with me if I was too solicitous. But it was precious time together for both of us. When we reached England, Ben went to stay with the W.s and I went to stay with Stephen and Mary. Ben had a wonderful time. Owen and Sophia were all over him. Catherine made sure he rested in the afternoon. Stephen and Mary hosted a wonderful farewell lunch at a restaurant on the 40th floor of a skyscraper with panoramic views of London. Ben linked arms with his cousins and their partners to drink cocktails.

When we returned to Australia, Anna was determined that Ben should not bleed to death from his bowel. She approached Ben's oncologist, Matt Carlino, who discussed it with Anna's former boss, surgeon Julie Howle. Julie Howle took Ben to surgery, was able to remove all three bowel lesions, and rejoin the bowel without the need for a colostomy. Anna took a week off work to sit by Ben's bedside and gently ensure that he got the best management as he recovered. I thanked Anna for looking after Ben so solicitously. She said: "I needed to do it for myself, Dad." For some weeks Ben's quality of life improved significantly. He was no longer bleeding and no longer needing frequent blood transfusions. But the melanoma was progressing, causing Ben a great deal of pain. He was transferred to a wonderful hospice, Naringah, for palliative care. There his pain relief was optimised. He could even enjoy his favourite drink, rum and Coke, thanks to a volunteer-run "Jolly Trolley" which did the rounds twice daily, offering drinks to patients and visitors. His brother Tom visited every day and built Lego characters with Ben. Mark, Tika and Tanah visited him. His adored and adoring cousin Catherine W. flew out from England to be with him. His faithful friend Hagan Slattery visited him almost every day. Ben's last weeks were as good as they could be. Ben died on April 1st 2023.

As Ben was dying, I developed a severe depressive illness, which put a huge load on Carmel, although Carmel is one of life's great copers. Every few days, Carmel drove me from the mental hospital where I was an inpatient to Naringah to visit Ben. Carmel organised Ben's funeral. She asked Ben's siblings to make a slide show of photographs of Ben. Carmel and all three siblings spoke at the funeral, which drew a huge crowd. They also organised for the funeral to be filmed and transmitted live, so that his English relatives and friends could watch it in real time. The wake was held in the garden of the pub where Ben used to do a trivia quiz each week. The pub served a complimentary round of rum and Coke to honour Ben.

I struggled throughout to cope with Ben's 7 year illness. When Ben was first diagnosed with melanoma, Carmel and I went for a coffee with Carmel's cousin, Mary Rennie, who is a publisher with HarperCollins. In the course of the conversation, Mary said I should write a book about all that immunisation has achieved. I had been a member of the national immunisation committee for 25 years. I said I had co-written a book on immunisation 10 years earlier with Gordon Ada,

Professor of Immunology at the Australian National University, and an erstwhile colleague of my father (Gordon's daughter Louise and her partner Rob are dear friends of ours). "Did anyone read it?" asked Mary. "Oh no", I admitted, "It was far too scientific for general consumption." Mary suggested I write a book for the public extolling the benefits of immunisation. I thought about it and decided the subject attracted me and it would help to stop me ruminating about Ben's illness. I drafted a list of chapters, including ethical issues, and started working on the first few chapters, which I sent to Mary Rennie. She and a young colleague at HarperCollins, Shannon Kelly, read them and came back with multiple suggestions. I was not used to this admirable level of scrutiny. Usually when I wrote a scientific book, I would present the publishers with a final product, which they would publish unchanged. Mary told me I should choose the two best chapters, and she would present them to a Board meeting, which had the say on whether or not HarperCollins would offer me a contract. With Mary's help I wrote two chapters. Apparently, at the Board meeting, the Chief Executive Officer of HarperCollins said "This is just my type of book", and all of a sudden the decision was unanimous. So I signed a contract and started writing the book, every evening after work and every free weekend. Working on the book certainly helped me to worry less about Ben. I found the creativity of thinking and writing very therapeutic. Mary was a wonderful editor and so was her colleague, Scott Forbes. I thought I would not have enough to say to fill the requisite 90,000 words. In the event I wrote 120,000. I needed to cut 30,000 words, but struggled to do so. HarperCollins commissioned Emma Dowden, known as "The Book Doctor", to do a surgical job on it. Maybe Emma should be renamed "The Book Surgeon". The book was much more succinct for Emma's work. I often read a book now and think it would have been better for a good editor. My book was published as *Defeating the Ministers of Death—The Compelling History of Vaccination*. The title derives from 17th century English historian,

Thomas Macaulay, who called smallpox "the most terrible of all the ministers of death". I thought it rather a clever title; that is, until I flew to Far North Queensland as an examiner and, in the airport bookshop, found my book in the War section. I have to admit that I surreptitiously moved it to the bestseller section. I was invited to speak at writers festivals in Brisbane (with my son Mark) and Canberra. I was interviewed by Richard Fidler for his popular radio programme *Conversations*, by Richard Glover for *Drive*, and by Norman Swan for *The Health Report*. I had my fifteen minutes of fame. My book was no bestseller, but I am ever so grateful to Mary Rennie who helped me get through a very difficult time.

David with Defeating the Ministries of Death

Book Launch at Gleebooks in Sydney

When Ben was dying, I had my first psychotic episode. I was 72 years old and nearing retirement. My father had his first psychotic episode at age 42, after a cerebral bleed. My identical twin brother Stephen had his first psychotic episode shortly before his 42nd birthday. When he was admitted to hospital, Stephen gave his name as Alick Isaacs. I am ashamed to admit that I had spent 30 years feeling rather smug at escaping my genetic destiny, and wondering what had been the protective factor. I suspected Carmel was the factor; nothing escapes Carmel. If I am nearing a breakdown ("wobbling" I call it), which happened once in Oxford and once more after I had been at a scientific meeting in China sleeping and eating poorly, Carmel persuades me to get psychiatric help in time to prevent a full breakdown. What was the cause or causes of my current psychotic depression? Was it Ben's terminal illness? Was it that I was nearing retirement? My mother made a serious suicidal attempt as she neared retirement and only survived because Stephen found her in the nick of time. After Susanna died and as she neared retirement, Harriet's mental health deteriorated. She was admitted to mental hospital and hated it. She travelled to the United States, I think to say a secret goodbye to her many friends there. Friends asked her if she was suicidal and Harriet said not. But, tragically she took her own life at age 60. Harriet had friends worldwide and was greatly loved. Her suicide hit her friends and family very hard, none more so than her loving husband Anthony and children Sam and Alice, who struggle to this day to cope with the loss. When someone commits suicide, friends and relatives agonise whether it could have been prevented. Suicide is brutally cruel.

Having a psychotic episode for me was like a bad dream. I remember getting the family in a circle around the oak tree in our garden and calling for a group hug. Our dear child psychiatrist friend Ken Nunn was wonderfully supportive of Carmel and me through this episode. My memories of what happened are very vague. Apparently my daughter Anna was incredibly influential in calling an ambulance when

I was too unwell to stay at home. I vaguely remember the ambulance and being strapped to a stretcher. What I don't remember is that, like my brother, I too told the ambulance driver that my name was Alick Isaacs. I remember being in a hospital Emergency Department, awake all night, watching what was happening. A man in a wheelchair kept doing laps of the ward and I waved to him every time he went past. I don't remember being transferred to the psychiatric hospital where I would spend the next few weeks.

I was transferred to a mental hospital shortly before Ben died. I needed electroconvulsive therapy (ECT). I had lost over 20 kilograms in weight. Was the weight loss all due to poor appetite or might there be an organic cause? An astute psychiatrist ordered an ultrasound of my abdomen, which showed that I had cancer of the head and tail of the pancreas with secondaries in the liver. There is a rare but recognised association between cancer of the head of the pancreas and severe depression. Was my depression caused, at least in part, by my cancer of the head of the pancreas? Was my pancreatic cancer a result of immune suppression caused by the stress of Ben's terminal illness? Fortunately, my depression responded well to the ECT. I was able to go home on lithium preventive therapy, but was exhausted a lot of the time. I have had radiotherapy to a lesion in my spine. I have had weeks of chemotherapy, which has helped my exhaustion, and allowed me to read (mainly re-reading Dickens, harking back to my mother's medical student days). As my pancreas fails, I have developed insulin-dependent diabetes. My friend, Craig Mellis, has been gently pushing me to write. Now that I am writing and enjoying it, he tells me there is scientific evidence, from a randomised controlled trial, that children with asthma who write do better clinically than asthmatics who do not write. I am getting great enjoyment from writing this memoir. So I can recommend writing for its therapeutic value.

This Christmas, my children gave me a subscription to a website, Storyworth, that encourages me to write short stories. Writing these short stories brings back memories, such as my trips with Carmel to Macchu Pichu, Galapagos, Rio and Antarctica. But I also feel encouraged to comment on my current situation: after reflecting on Alesandr Solzhenitsyn's book *Cancer* Ward, written after he was diagnosed with testicular cancer, I have just completed an essay on what it is like attending the Cancer Chemotherapy Ward at Westmead Hospital.

When I retired I was given the honour of being awarded the prestigious 2024 annual Howard Williams medal of the Paediatrics and Health Division of the Royal Australasian College of Physicians. In addition, the Australasian Society for Infectious Diseases (ASID) did me the extraordinary honour of creating a new annual commemorative medal in Health and Humanity, named in my honour and with me as the first recipient in 2025. In my acceptance speech I mentioned how my geriatrician uncle Bernard Isaacs had been famous for the describing the four I's of social geriatrics: intellect (cerebral dysfunction), incontinence, immobility and instability (falls). My comparable advice was that paediatricians should aspire to be be interested in patients and their families, should be inquisitive about their lives, while remaining respectful about how to approach the families: two I's and an R instead of Bernard's four I's.

I feel as if I have had a fortunate life. I was loved by my parents as a child, surely the greatest gift that any child can receive. I am married to a wonderful woman, whom I adore. I have had four successful children and 5 adorable and fascinating grandchildren. Carmel and I have had to cope with tragedy: the loss of my father Alick at age 45, of Carmel's brother Billy at age 25, the loss of my sister at age 60, and the loss of our son Ben at age 42 were blows from which we have never totally recovered. On the positive side, our three remaining children are making a name for themselves and making a difference in the world, and I am immensely proud of them (as I was of Ben).

All my life, since childhood, I have wondered what it would be like to be dying. In the past, poets romanticised dying young from consumption (tuberculosis). The truth is, as shown by the death of John Keats, that death from consumption was ghastly. My lifelong dream was to learn I had a fatal but painless disease, which would allow me sufficient time to say farewells to my family and friends. In this I am remarkably fortunate. I will die soon from pancreatic cancer, but I have had no pain, only minimal drug-induced nausea. I have had adequate time to say fond farewells to those family and friends I love most in the world. When my children asked me my feelings about my illness, I said I didn't want to discuss it with them. "It is what it is."

Mark and Tika's wedding, 2023

FAREWELL MY FRIENDS
BY RABINDRANATH TAGORE

It was beautiful
As long as it lasted
The journey of my life.

I have no regrets
Whatsoever save
The pain I'll leave behind.

Those dear hearts
Who love and care
And the heavy with sleep
Ever moist eyes
The smile inspite of a
Lump in the throat
And the strings pulling
At the heart and soul.

The strong arms
That held me up
When my own strength
Let me down
Each morsel that I was
Fed with was full of love divine.

At every turning of my life
I came across
Good friends
Friends who stood by me
Even when time raced me by.

Farewell
Farewell
My friends
I smile and bid you goodbye
No, shed no tears
For I need them not
All I need is your smile.

If you feel sad
Do think of me
For that's what I'll like
When you live in the hearts
Of those you love
Remember then ...
You never die.

DAVID ISAACS

23 Sept 1950 – 02 Aug 2025

ACKNOWLEDGEMENTS

I thank my belovèd wife Carmel. In *Defeating the Ministers of Death*, I refer to Carmel as the lodestone of my existence, a reference to a poem by Rabindranath Tagore. I don't think I can express any better how much I owe to Carmel and how much I love her.

I thank my wonderful children, including Ben. I am immensely proud of all of them. I thank them, too, for having such adorable children. It is wonderful being a grandfather, and being able to hand the children back at the end of the day.

I thank my brother Stephen and his wife Mary, who have been incredibly close and loving to us over the years. I thank their children and their children's partners and their children's children for the love and support they showed Ben.

I thank my late parents for giving us a loving start in life.

I thank my wonderful child psychiatrist friend, Ken Nunn, for his loving support of Carmel and me through my psychotic illness.

I thank my psychiatrists, Philip Mitchell and Philip Boyce, my oncologist Adnan Nagrial and my palliative care physician Jus Rakhra for their excellent care.

I thank my teachers, whether they be my mentors Bernie Valman and Richard Moxon, my school teachers from kindergarten onward, university teachers, or colleagues from whom I have learnt so much and who I have tried to emulate.

I thank Mark and Tom Isaacs for extensive comments on a previous manuscript, most of which I heeded, and I especially thank wonderful Mary Rennie for finding time to copy edit this manuscript.

I thank all those mentioned in this book, too numerous to name here, for their friendship and care.

REFERENCES

1. Foss HJ. *Music in my Time*. London, Rich & Cowan: 1933.
2. Staliūnas D. Enemies for a day: Antisemitism and anti-Jewish violence in Lithuania under the Tsars. *Lithuanian Historical Studies*; 2016: 20 (1): 268–274. DOI: 10.30965/25386565-02001017.
3. Andrewes CH. Obituary of Alick Isaacs. *Biographical Memoirs of Fellows of the Royal Society* 1967; 13: 204–221. Link: royalsocietypublishing.org/doi/epdf/10.1098/rsbm.1967.0010 (accessed 12.11.24).
4. Isaacs D. Feminism, equity and the family-centred workplace. *Journal of Paediatrics and Child Health* 2019; 55: 497–8.
5. Young M. *The Elmhirsts of Dartington. The Creation of an Utopian Community*. London, Routledge & Kegan Hall, 1982.
6. Dutta K, Robinson B. Rabindranath Tagore. The Myriad-Minded Man. London, Bloomsbury: 1995.
7. Brent LB. *Susanna Isaacs-Elmhirst obituary*. The Guardian, April 29th, 2010. Link: theguardian.com/society/2010/apr/29/susanna-isaacs-elmhirst-obituary (accessed 12.11.24).
8. Isaacs D, Fitzgerald D. Seven alternatives to evidence-based medicine. *BMJ* 1999; 319: 1618. DOI: 10.1136/bmj.319.7225.1618

COPYRIGHT

First published in 2025 by Ligature Pty Limited

PO Box 294 · Balmain NSW 2041 · Australia
www.ligatu.re · mail@ligatu.re

Hardcover ISBN 978-1-922749-99-4
Paperback ISBN 978-1-923146-02-0
e-book ISBN 978-1-923146-03-7

ligaturefirst

www.ingramcontent.com/pod-product-compliance
Lightning Source LLC
Chambersburg PA
CBHW061235070526
44584CB00030B/4140
9781923146020